THE ASSYRIANS AND THE BABYLONIANS

HISTORY AND TREASURES OF AN ANCIENT CIVILIZATION

WHITE STAR PUBLISHERS

CONTENTS

1

2

3

TEXTS
ALFREDO RIZZA

EDITORIAL DIRECTOR
VALERIA MANFERTO DE FABIANIS

COLLABORATING EDITORS
LAURA ACCOMAZZO
GIORGIO FERRERO

GRAPHIC DESIGNER
PAOLA PIACCO

© 2007 White Star s.p.a.
Via Candido Sassone, 22/24
13100 Vercelli, Italy
www.whitestar.it

TRANSLATION: RICHARD PIERCE

ISBN: 978-88-544-0268-3

REPRINTS:
1 2 3 4 5 6   11 10 09 08 07
Color separation: Fotomec, Turin
Printed in China

1 - THIS BULL WITH A HUMAN HEAD (H. 420 CM) ONCE STOOD AT THE ENTRANCE OF THE PALACE OF SARGON II (MUSÉE DU LOUVRE, PARIS).

2-3 - THE STANDARD OF UR (H. 20 CM) DATES FROM THE MID-III MILLENNIUM BC (BRITISH MUSEUM, LONDON).

4-5 - IN THIS I MILLENNIUM BC ASSYRIAN RELIEF SCULPTURE (H. 192 CM), ELAMITE SOLDIERS ARE MARCHING AGAINST ASSURBANIPAL (BRITISH MUSEUM, LONDON).

6-7 - THE RECONSTRUCTION OF THE GATE OF ISHTAR (VORDERASIATISCHES MUSEUM, BERLIN).

9 - IMDUGUD, THE LION-HEADED EAGLE (H. 12.8 CM), COMES FROM THE SO-CALLED TREASURE OF UR, FROM MARI (NATIONAL MUSEUM, DAMASCUS).

INTRODUCTION

The history, myths and achievements of the Assyrians and Babylonians have always stirred awe in us for their ancientness, splendor and power, as well as for the mark these people have left on the history of Man. The abandonment of cities that were once grandiose and the overlapping of various different cultures have contributed to the creation of a progressive and inexorable dilution of historic memory that resulted, not too many decades ago, in a concept of Assyro-Babylonian culture and history that is often obscure, not well defined, decidedly mythological and, in some cases, absolutely wrong. Western tradition has handed down episodes that for the most part have been reduced to anecdotes in that their cultural context are wholly different from the original ones and no longer represent valid historic documentation. Certainly, the Greeks, Romans and the Jewish-Christian world have contributed a great deal to creating this idea of the Middle East as "effete," luxurious and licentious on the one hand and as a terrifying, evil and cruel executor of divine punishment on the other, and the breakdown of tradition and of the preservation of works dedicated to the Orient in antiquity resulted in a definitive "black hole" in documentation, casting a permanent shadow over the truth about the culture of those distant nations.

With the resumption of relations between East and West in the second part of the Middle Ages and then in the modern age, interest in the ancient Near and Middle East also grew, and in the 17th and 18th centuries original documents began to arrive in Europe from their original sources. Pietro della Valle, a Roman aristocratic engaged in long "pilgrimages" throughout the Near and Middle East, sent reports of impressive ruins and characters of a mysterious and fascinating writing system. Other travelers were deeply impressed by the ruins of the ancient Persian cities and contributed to different degrees to the birth of the discipline known as Assyriology. Here mention will be made of only a few extremely important persons, such as Carsten Niebuhr, the 18th-century geographer who provided prodigious documentation regarding Near Eastern antiquity and identified Nineveh, near modern-day Mossul. In the early 19th century Georg Friedrich Grotefend, a classics school teacher from Göttingen, laid the foundations for the decipherment of cuneiform script, a technique that was later perfected by several scholars, the most charismatic of whom was certainly Henry C. Rawlinson. Others who devoted their energy to research on and documentation of Near Eastern antiquity were not only academics but also merchants, diplomats and artists. In the last-mentioned group was Robert Kerr Porter, who made virtually perfect drawings of the ruins he came upon during his journeys. A physician also became famous as the discoverer of the impressive ruins of Khorsabad, the capital of King Sargon II: Paul Emile Botta. He was followed by Austen H. Layard, Hormuzd Rassam, Robert Koldewey and Walter Andrae, who, through the excavations of Nineveh, Nimrud, Babylon and Assur succeeded in removing the veil that had concealed so many marvelous treasures. The archaeological discoveries and the decipherment of cuneiform documents led to an exponential increase in data and to the discovery of entire civilizations, such as the Sumerian, which had remained in a state of utter oblivion.

The increase in our knowledge then made it necessary to divide the various sectors of research. Thus, in the strict sense, the expression "Assyro-Babylonian civilization" indicates the complex of historic events, facts and personages that were pivotal in the development of Mesopotamia in the II and I Millennium BC (ca. 2000–500 BC).

10 - THE UPPER PART OF THE STELE OF HAMMURABI (H. 88 INCHES/225 CM), ON WHICH ARE CARVED THE LAW CODES OF THIS FAMOUS OLD BABYLONIAN RULER (MUSÉE DU LOUVRE, PARIS).

11 - THE ROARING LION WITH A SOLEMN GAIT WAS A TYPICAL MOTIF IN THE MONUMENTAL CONSTRUCTIONS OF BABYLON UNDER NEBUCHADNEZZAR II (VORDERASIATISCHES MUSEUM, BERLIN).

However, it must be said that the origins of all the above date back to the preceding millennium (3000–2001 BC), a period that witnessed the rise of the Sumerian and Akkadian civilizations. It should therefore come as no surprise that the first major feature of Assyro-Babylonian civilization, the one that most stimulates our intellectual curiosity as well as our imagination, is its ancientness. The name "Mesopotamia" derives from that fact that it is the "land between rivers," that is, between the Tigris and the Euphrates, which corresponds to modern-day Iraq.

The Sumerians produced the first civilization attested by written documents in a region of southern Mesopotamia that is now in the present-day province-governorate of Dhi Qar (Nassiriyah). We do not know where the Sumerians came from, and the language they spoke is not related to any other known tongue. The region further north was settled by the Akkadians, a population that spoke a Semitic language, Akkadian, which is related to languages that are still spoken, such as Arabic, Aramaic and Hebrew. In a later period Akkadian split up into two regional varieties: Assyrian was spoken in the north, between Mosul and Kirkuk, while in the south, the provinces of Diyala, Baghdad, Babil and other outlying provinces spoke Babylonian. The Akkadian-speaking people dominated those who spoke Sumerian. In particular, the Akkadians of the south, the Babylonians, replaced the Sumerians, who handed down their language and literature to the new conquerors. Consequently, Sumerian became a language of educated people, somewhat similar to what happened with Latin in Europe.

The history of Assyria and Babylonia is characterized by a wide variety and range of historic events and a rather complex political-cultural configuration. In Mesopotamia several ethnic-cultural groups came into play. There were the Amorites, Aramaeans, Chaldaeans and other western Semitic peoples who were semi-nomadic and whose society had an aristocratic structure. The Hurrites and other populations for the most part from mountain regions came from the north, and the Hittites and Urartians from Turkey. From the east came the Kassites and the Indo-Aryan elite of Mitanni, the populations from the Zagros Mts. such as the Lullubìti and the Guti, and the Elamites, whose nucleus lay in Susiana, which is in present-day Khuzistan

(Iran). A special and, everything considered, rather modest role was played by Egypt, with which Mesopotamia often had intense trade and diplomatic relations but relatively little cultural and military contact, at least up to the I Millennium BC.

Although it survived up to the beginning of the Christian era, the Assyro-Babylonian civilization ceased being politically independent in 539 BC, when the Persians under Cyrus the Great conquered Babylon and set about establishing one of the greatest empires in history, which unified under more or less direct control the Middle and Near East and extended its political and cultural influence to the Mediterranean. Persian culture took on many features of Babylonian civilization and was a mediator between the Near East and the world of Greek culture. The heritage of Babylonia survived through Greek and Roman culture, but this legacy became more and more remote and over the centuries it was above all the Bible that narrated the vicissitudes and features of a civilization that, as we have seen, no longer corresponded to historical reality.

One of the most important problems that scholars of Near Eastern history have to face is the total lack of stable and certain chronology in this field. For the III and II millennia the dates must not only be considered somewhat approximate, but conventional as well. Thanks to some texts that have been dated to the age of Ammi-Saduqa, the king of the first dynasty of Babylon (17th century BC), which contain observations regarding the planet Venus, scholars have formulated hypothetical chronological reconstructions with absolute dates. But because of the characteristics of the phenomena described in the texts, it was possible only to indicate a time range in which these phenomena should have occurred. Thus we have a "maximum" date, the most ancient one, on the basis of which scholars have constructed what is termed the *long chronology*, and there is a more recent "minimum" date used as the basis for the *short chronology*. The intermediate date provides the point of reference for the *median chronology*, which is the one I have decided to utilize in this book whenever indicating absolute dates. The differences are by no means slight. For example, the dates for Hammurabi of Babylon are 1848–1806 BC according to the long chronology, 1792–1750 BC according to the median one and 1728–1686 BC according to the short one.

CHRONOLOGY

THE ORIGINS
(10,000–3500 BC)

During the Neolithic, the populations along the Fertile Crescent began to exploit plant and animal resources more intensively. Around 7500 BC the "agricultural revolution" began, creating the ideal conditions for a great population increase. The Chalcolithic (4500–3500 BC) is marked by the increasing use made of metals and alloys such as copper and bronze and by the rise of the first large villages.

THE EARLY BRONZE AGE
(3500–2000 BC)

The period from 3100 to 2900 BC marked the rise of the so-called urban revolution. The invention of writing made it possible to manage and move large numbers of objects and men. The "grand organizations" (temples and palaces) were able to plan and build enormous monumental centers and grandiose works of irrigation and land management. The Sumerians gained control of Mesopotamia during the Proto-Dynastic period (2900–2350 BC). The first Akkadian civilization rose up, with the extraordinary experience of the Akkad Empire, which ruled from 2350 to 2150 BC. After the interregnum of the "barbarian" populations of Gutium, in 2100 BC Ur-Nammu gave rise to the "Sumerian rebirth" with the Ur III Dynasty (2100–2000 BC).

THE MIDDLE BRONZE AGE
(2000–1600 BC)

The Sumerian civilization was incorporated into the Akkadian one, now represented to the north by the Assyrians and to the south by the Babylonians. The Amaraean (Old Babylonian) civilizations fight for hegemony: between Babylonia, Larsa and Eshnunna the first-mentioned emerged victorious thanks to the action of Hammurabi (1792–1750), whose dynasty lasted until 1600 BC, after which the Kassites took control. Assyria witnessed the rise of the Old Assyrian society.

THE LATE BRONZE AGE
(1600–1200 BC)

The transition from the Middle to the Late Bronze Age was marked by crucial changes on a social and ethnic level. Babylon became the true cultural center of the region. A system of international relations was created, centered around the reciprocal recognition of ruling powers ("great kingdoms") and vassal states ("minor kingdoms"). From around 1400 BC Babylon was subjugated by the Assyrian state, whose power grew until it demanded control of Babylon itself (Middle Assyrian Kingdom). The "light chariot" and other military innovations became widespread, contributing to the formation of increasingly influential military elites.

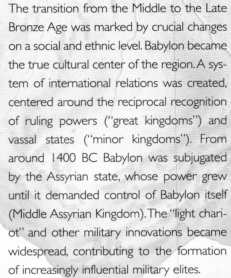

THE IRON AGE
(1200–539 BC)

Between the II and I Millennium the introduction of new techniques for the extraction and processing of iron accompanied a period of crucial political and social changes. The late Bronze Age powers collapsed. From about 750 BC the policy of Tiglath-pileser III brought about the birth of the Neo-Assyrian Empire. The Aramaean "nations" spread the new Aramaic alphabet and language in the Near and Middle East. The Assyrian civilization produced impressive achievements in the capitals Kalakh (Ashurnasirpal II 883–859 BC), and Dur Sharrukin (Sargon II, 721–705). Sennacherib (704–681) turned Nineveh into the "incomparable" capital and destroyed Babylon. During the reign of Esarhaddon (680–669) and Ashurbanipal (668–630 ca.) the Assyrians attempted to absorb and develop all Babylonian literary and scientific production. Babylon was rebuilt by Esarhaddon. The sudden fall of the empire shortly after the year 630 BC was followed by the reemergence of Babylonian supremacy under the Chaldean kings Nabopolassar (625–605) and Nebuchadnezzar II (604–562). Nabonedo (555–539), was defeated by Cyrus II the Great.

BLACK SEA

HATTUSHASH

ARMENIA

CAPPADOCIA

KÜLTEPE

ARSLAN TASH
TELL AHMAR

TELL HALA
TELL LEILAN
TELL BRAK

EBLA

UGARIT

MARI

ARABIAN
PENINSULA

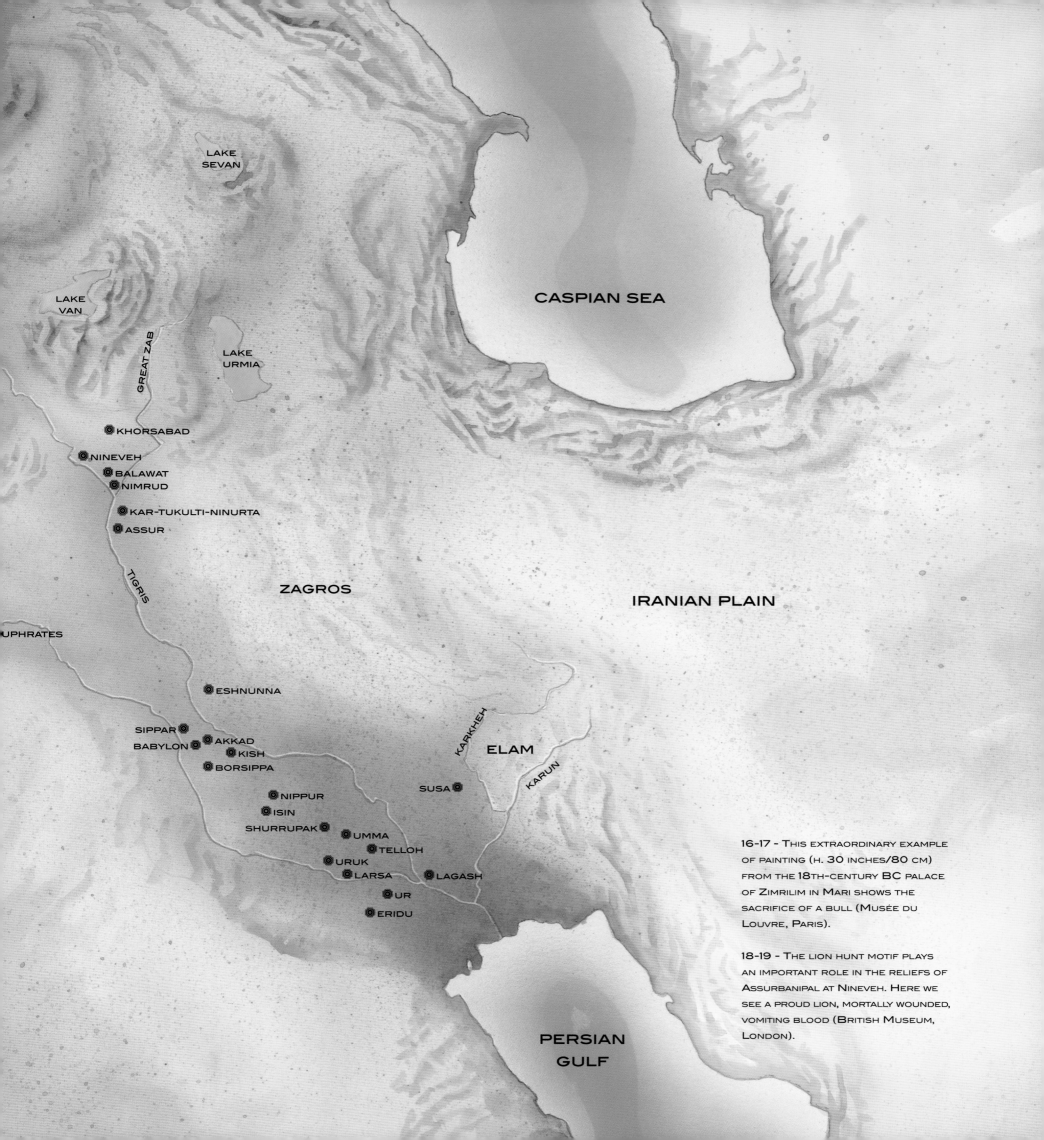

LAKE
SEVAN

CASPIAN SEA

LAKE
VAN

LAKE
URMIA

GREAT ZAB

◎ KHORSABAD

◎ NINEVEH
◎ BALAWAT
◎ NIMRUD

◎ KAR-TUKULTI-NINURTA

◎ ASSUR

TIGRIS

ZAGROS

IRANIAN PLAIN

UPHRATES

◎ ESHNUNNA

SIPPAR ◎
BABYLON ◎ ◎ AKKAD
◎ KISH
◎ BORSIPPA

KARKHEH

ELAM

◎ NIPPUR
◎ ISIN
SHURRUPAK ◎ ◎ UMMA
◎ TELLOH
◎ URUK
◎ LARSA ◎ LAGASH
◎ UR
◎ ERIDU

SUSA ◎

KARUN

16-17 - THIS EXTRAORDINARY EXAMPLE
OF PAINTING (H. 30 INCHES/80 CM)
FROM THE 18TH-CENTURY BC PALACE
OF ZIMRILIM IN MARI SHOWS THE
SACRIFICE OF A BULL (MUSÉE DU
LOUVRE, PARIS).

18-19 - THE LION HUNT MOTIF PLAYS
AN IMPORTANT ROLE IN THE RELIEFS OF
ASSURBANIPAL AT NINEVEH. HERE WE
SEE A PROUD LION, MORTALLY WOUNDED,
VOMITING BLOOD (BRITISH MUSEUM,
LONDON).

PERSIAN
GULF

1

MESOPOTAMIA AT THE DAWN OF CIVILIZATION AND IN THE II MILLENNIUM

THE BIRTH OF CIVILIZATION

Long before the Assyrian rulers and their fearsome armies devastated Palestine, leaving an indelible mark in the Bible, the cradle of Mesopotamian civilization, the creative and organizational center of power and knowledge that were destined to last for thousands of years, was a "new" land facing the Persian Gulf and open to natural expansion northwards, a territory that was the birthplace of a network of cities later known as the Land of Sumer.

More than 5000 years ago this region was rather hostile to human habitation because of the overabundant presence of water and the floods of the two great rivers, which at that time were beyond the people's ability to manage. During the Neolithic period (10,000–3500 BC), evidence of the first important inventions in agriculture and animal husbandry and the rise of large villages can be found all along the slopes of the Zagros mountain range (between Iraq and Iran) and the Taurus Mts. (between Iraq, Iran and Turkey), as well as in Lebanon and Palestine. If we were to visualize all thes hilly regions as if they were united into a single imaginary line, they would trace the arc of the so-called Fertile Crescent.

During the late Neolithic (6000–3500 BC), important developments, particularly in the field of technology, spread throughout this region. The Mesopotamian populations gradually felt the urgent need for more space in order to exploit the innovations that allowed them to cultivate cereals intensively and to develop to the full a new social tendency – specialization in work and social roles. In effect, this period witnessed the creation of society as we see it today, that is, a complex of persons who, occupying different roles and hierarchies, contributed to the growth of the group as a whole. These crucial changes accompanied the establishment of new forms of settlement and communal life—the large villages and networks of villages that would later give rise to the city system with its typical stratification of social roles and positions. However, this was not yet the period of development of Lower Mesopotamia, but rather of the territory east of the Zagros range, where Susiana is located. Susiana is the region that gave birth to a very ancient culture that was a vital part of the history of the Near and Middle East, the so-called Elamite civilization. The region was named after its most important city, Susa, which remained prominent for thousands of years, up to the rise of the Persian Empire (539–323 BC), of which it would become one of the capitals. The Susiana territory (now in Iran) was, geographically speaking, quite suitable for development of the first cities, but soon Susa was surpassed by Sumer as the center of progress and power in the development of the city-state.

21 - A DIORITE SCULPTURE PORTRAYING THE NEO-SUMERIAN KING OF LAGASH, GUDEA (H. 9 INCHES/23 CM; MUSÉE DU LOUVRE, PARIS).

22 AND 23 TOP RIGHT - THE ARTISTIC PRODUCTION OF THE NEOLITHIC ERA INCLUDES FEMALE FIGURINES THAT MAY HAVE BEEN CONNECTED WITH FERTILITY CULTS (H. 3.25 INCHES/8.3 CM; MUSÉE DU LOUVRE, PARIS).

23 TOP LEFT - THE NEOLITHIC FEMALE FIGURES SEEM TO HAVE BEEN ALMOST ALWAYS LINKED TO REPRODUCTION. THE STATUETTES MIGHT REPRESENT DIVINITIES OR VOTIVE OBJECTS (H. 5.5 INCHES/13.8 CM; BRITISH MUSEUM, LONDON).

23 BOTTOM - ANIMALS, AND CATTLE IN PARTICULAR, PLAYED A CENTRAL ROLE IN THE ECONOMY AND CULTURE OF THE NEAR EAST FROM THE TIME OF THE "NEOLITHIC REVOLUTION" ON (H. 2.25 INCHES/5.9 CM; MUSÉE DU LOUVRE, PARIS).

24 LEFT - THIS VASE IS AN EXAMPLE OF THE NEIGHBORING SUSIAN STYLE (III MILLENNIUM BC), WHICH COMBINES NATURALISM AND GEOMETRIC FORMS. THERE IS A DIVISION INTO REGISTERS THAT CORRESPOND TO THE VARIOUS PARTS OF THE OBJECT, ONE OF WHICH IS AGAIN DIVIDED INTO FIELDS OR SECTORS (MUSÉE DU LOUVRE, PARIS).

24 RIGHT - THE PREHISTORIC CULTURE OF SUSA DEVELOPED IN THE SAME PERIOD AS MESOPOTAMIAN CULTURE, WITH WHICH IT COMPETED ON AN EQUAL FOOTING. THE STYLISTIC FEATURES ARE QUITE SIMILAR TO THOSE OF THE CONTEMPORANEOUS HALAF CULTURE, AS CAN BE SEEN IN THIS IV MILLENNIUM BC OBJECT (MUSÉE DU LOUVRE, PARIS).

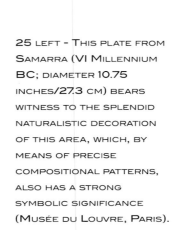

25 LEFT - THIS PLATE FROM SAMARRA (VI MILLENNIUM BC; DIAMETER 10.75 INCHES/27.3 CM) BEARS WITNESS TO THE SPLENDID NATURALISTIC DECORATION OF THIS AREA, WHICH, BY MEANS OF PRECISE COMPOSITIONAL PATTERNS, ALSO HAS A STRONG SYMBOLIC SIGNIFICANCE (MUSÉE DU LOUVRE, PARIS).

25 RIGHT - HIGHLY REFINED DECORATIVE TECHNIQUE WAS A CHARACTERISTIC FEATURE OF THE CERAMICS OF THE HALAF CULTURE (VI–V MILLENNIUM BC), WHICH WAS PARTLY CONTEMPORANEOUS WITH THE CULTURE OF SAMARRA. HERE IS A MAGNIFICENT EXAMPLE (DIAMETER 6.25 INCHES/16 CM) FROM ARPACHIYA (MUSÉE DU LOUVRE, PARIS).

26 TOP - THE SO-CALLED PROTO-URBAN PERIOD (3300–3000 BC) OF SUSA WAS MARKED BY THE RISE OF A COMPLEX CIVILIZATION THAT PRODUCED, AMONG OTHER THINGS, THESE CYLINDRICAL SEALS (H. 1.50 INCHES/3.9 CM; MUSÉE DU LOUVRE, PARIS).

26 BOTTOM LEFT - THANKS TO THE IMPRESSIONS ON THE SEALS, WE ARE ACQUAINTED WITH MANY ASPECTS OF EVERYDAY LIFE, SUCH AS IN THIS EXAMPLE FROM THE SUSA EXCAVATIONS (H. 1.50 INCHES/3.8 CM; MUSÉE DU LOUVRE, PARIS).

26 BOTTOM RIGHT - DURING THE SO-CALLED PROTO-URBAN PERIOD, TEMPLES WERE EXTREMELY IMPORTANT IN THE SUSA AREA, AS CAN BE SEEN BY THIS CYLINDRICAL SEAL (MUSÉE DU LOUVRE, PARIS).

27 - THIS RELIEF (H. 7.75 INCHES/20 CM) GIVES US AN IDEA OF THE REPRESENTATION OF CULT SCENES TYPICAL OF THE SUSA REGION IN THE III MILLENNIUM BC: TWO FIGURES ARE MAKING RITUAL GESTURES TO A MARVELOUS DOUBLE SERPENT THAT IS BITING ITS TAIL (MUSÉE DU LOUVRE, PARIS).

28 - BUILDINGS IN THE NEAR EAST, BOTH IN MESOPOTAMIA AND SUSA, HAD STONE PLAQUES LIKE THIS ONE (H. 6.50 INCHES/17 CM) FIXED TO THEIR WALLS, SOMEWHAT NEAR THE DOORS. IN THE MIDDLE WAS A PEG ON WHICH WERE ATTACHED ROPES USED TO KEEP THE DOORS CLOSED (MUSÉE DU LOUVRE, PARIS).

29 - THIS STATUETTE (H.6 INCHES/14.8 CM) REVEALS STRIKING SIMILARITIES BETWEEN MESOPOTAMIAN AND SUSIAN ART. THE POSITION OF THE HANDS AND THE GARMENT COVERING ONLY ONE SHOULDER WERE ALSO TYPICAL MOTIFS OF MESOPOTAMIAN PORTRAITS, WHICH OFTEN REPRESENTED HIGH-RANKING PERSONAGES (MUSÉE DU LOUVRE, PARIS).

SUMER: WRITING AND POWER

Around 3500 BC Lower Mesopotamia gradually gained the upper hand over the surrounding areas. The populations created true networks of villages, some of which developed into cities because of their religious, administrative and military importance, which can be noted above all in the monuments that have survived. Uruk was the most important of these cities, but mention should also be made of Eridu, Ur, Kish, Umma and Larsa. Beyond the Zagros range

Susa still reigned supreme, but other cities spread eastward.

In a very short time (3000–2900 BC) the new Mesopotamian culture created, or better, invented the city, the state and a writing system. The population increased enormously compared to 3500 BC, thanks mostly to the intensive cultivation of cereals, the early forms of irrigation canal construction, the organization of the land into fields and, more generally speaking, the great availability of energy resources. In this early stage the Sumerians (this is the name we use for the people of the "land of Sumer") had enough manual labor at their disposal to build large monuments, such as temples and palaces. They were able to manage

the large quantity of goods they had accumulated and to organize the distribution of food and tools as well as assign tasks and responsibility, thanks to an innovation of crucial importance in the history of humanity – writing.

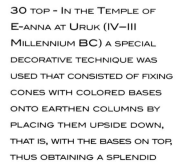

30 TOP - IN THE TEMPLE OF E-ANNA AT URUK (IV–III MILLENNIUM BC) A SPECIAL DECORATIVE TECHNIQUE WAS USED THAT CONSISTED OF FIXING CONES WITH COLORED BASES ONTO EARTHEN COLUMNS BY PLACING THEM UPSIDE DOWN, THAT IS, WITH THE BASES ON TOP, THUS OBTAINING A SPLENDID MOSAIC EFFECT.

30 BOTTOM - THIS DETAIL OF THE SO-CALLED STONE BUILDING FROM URUK (IV MILLENNIUM BC) ILLUSTRATES THE MASSIVENESS OF THE WALLS AS WELL AS THE REGULAR LAYOUT. THE FUNCTION OF THE CONSTRUCTION IS STILL WRAPPED IN MYSTERY; SOME SCHOLARS SAY IT WAS USED FOR BURIALS.

30-31 - A PHOTOGRAPH OF AN INTERESTING VIEW OF THE E-ANNA COMPLEX AT URUK (IV–III MILLENNIUM BC). URUK WAS CONSIDERED THE "FIRST CITY," IN THE TRUE SENSE OF THE WORD, IN HISTORY, PARTLY BECAUSE WRITING MAY HAVE BEEN INVENTED THERE.

31 CENTER LEFT - THE WHITE TEMPLE IN THE MIDDLE OF THE KULLAB AREA IN URUK DATES FROM THE LATE IV MILLENNIUM BC.

31 CENTER MIDDLE - THE STATELY AND ELEGANT CONSTRUCTION OF THE LATE IV MILLENNIUM BC BUILDINGS IN E-ANNA HAS LED SCHOLARS TO BELIEVE THAT THEY WERE TEMPLES.

31 CENTER RIGHT - THE SO-CALLED STONE BUILDING WAS FOUND RECENTLY IN THE KULLAB ZONE, THAT IS TO SAY, AT THE BASE OF THE ZIGGURAT OF AN IN URUK, WHICH DATES TO THE LATE IV MILLENNIUM BC.

31 BOTTOM - A PHOTOGRAPH WITH AN OVERALL VIEW OF A SECTION OF DIGS OF THE MOST IMPORTANT PROTO-HISTORIC SITE IN MESOPOTAMIA—URUK.

32 LEFT - THIS STYLIZED TERRA-COTTA IDOL (H. 10.50 INCHES/27 CM) ACCENTUATES WHAT PROBABLY REPRESENTS THE EYES. THERE ARE OTHER SIMILAR EXAMPLES FROM THE "EYE TEMPLE" AT TELL BRAK (MUSÉE DU LOUVRE, PARIS).

32 RIGHT - THIS STONE RECEPTACLE FROM URUK (H. 8 INCHES/20.3 CM) HAS A SCENE IN WHICH A LION, A SACRED ANIMAL OF INANA (AT LEFT IS THE PROFILE), IS ATTACKING TWO BULLS, WHILE TWO OTHER LIONS DOMINATE THE RELIEF (IRAQ MUSEUM, BAGHDAD).

33 RIGHT - THIS RITUAL VASE OR CUP (H. 5.50 INCHES/14.2 CM) FROM URUK REPRESENTS A BATTLE BETWEEN BULLS AND A LION (IV MILLENNIUM BC; BRITISH MUSEUM, LONDON).

33 LEFT - A LOVELY STONE VASE WITH ANIMALS (H. 4.75 INCHES/12 CM) DATING FROM THE LATE URUK PERIOD (LATE IV MILLENNIUM BC; BRITISH MUSEUM, LONDON).

34 LEFT – THIS STATUETTE (H. 10 INCHES/25 CM) OF A BEAREDED NUDE MAN WITH HIS HANDS IN THE CHARACTERISTIC POSITION IS AN EXAMPLE OF ARCHAIC SCULPTURE (IV MILLENNIUM BC) THAT WAS STILL RENDERED BY MEANS OF CYLINDRICAL VOLUMES (MUSÉE DU LOUVRE, PARIS).

34 RIGHT – ON THIS OBJECT (LENGTH **6.25** INCHES/15.9 CM), WHICH PROBABLY DATES FROM THE END OF THE IV MILLENNIUM BC, ARE SOME LETTERS, AMONG WHICH, ABOVE THE FIGURE SEATED AT LEFT, ARE THE STAR THAT INDICATES DIVINITIES AND THE CHARACTER THAT STANDS FOR FEMALE (BRITISH MUSEUM, LONDON).

35 – AN ALABASTER BUST OF A NUDE MAN (H. **7** INCHES/18 CM) DATING FROM THE LATE URUK PERIOD, BETWEEN THE IV AND III MILLENNIUM BC. THIS SCULPTURE ALREADY REVEALS THE SPECIAL ATTENTION PAID BY THE ARTIST TO ANATOMICAL DETAIL, ABOVE ALL IN THE RENDERING OF THE MUSCLES (IRAQ MUSEUM, BAGHDAD).

Writing was one of the most important, if not the most important, cultural factors in Mesopotamia. Known as cuneiform writing, because of the wedge-like form of the characters impressed on tablets of wet clay, on stone statues and on rock, this script lasted for over 3000 years and influenced the literature and even the mythology of its inventors.

The writing system invented in Sumer spread throughout the Near East. To the east, the Elamite civilization, an offshoot of the Susa civilization, assimilated the new invention and added its own original features. To the north, cuneiform script was adopted first by the Akkadians (Assyrians and Babylonians), and then by the Hurrites, the Hittites in Anatolia and, later on, by a population known as the Urartians. In the western regions, Mesopotamian script was used by the Semitic populations of Ebla and the "land of Amurru," which in the terminology of the time indicated Syria and Palestine.

Thanks to the invention of writing and the widespread use made of it in the various kingdoms of Mesopotamia in the III Millennium, we now have many documents on which to base our studies of the history and culture of those ancient peoples. In a span of one thousand years there was a long series of leading nations: the Sumerians in the so-called Proto-Dynastic period; the Akkadians in the great kingdom of Akkad founded by the famous King Sargon; an intermediate period characterized by "barbarian" invasions; and lastly, the "Sumerian rebirth" marked by the foundation of the Kingdom of Ur, known among specialists as the Ur III or Third Dynasty of Ur.

36 TOP LEFT - THIS DOCUMENT CONTAINS A LIST OF NAMES (H. 1.75 INCHES/4.4 CM; MUSÉE DU LOUVRE, PARIS).

36 TOP RIGHT - AT LEFT IN THIS TABLET (H. 3 INCHES/7.4 CM) IS THE CHARACTER FOR "BEER" (MUSÉE DU LOUVRE, PARIS).

36 CENTER - A TABLET (H. 3.75 INCHES/9.4 CM) WITH THE REGISTRATION OF BEER (BRITISH MUSEUM. LONDON).

36 BOTTOM - THIS TABLET SHOWS THE EVOLUTION OF CUNEIFORM CHARACTERS.

37 - AN ECONOMIC DOCUMENT DATING BACK TO 2500 BC (H. 3.25 INCHES/8.5 CM; MUSÉE DU LOUVRE, PARIS).

LATE URUK CA. 3100 BC	GEMDET NASR- CA. 3000 BC	PRE-DYNASTIC III CA. 2400 BC	UR III CA. 2000 BC	MEANING
				SAG HEAD
				NINDA BREAD
				KÚ TO EAT
				ÁB COW
				APIN PLOW
				KI EARTH, PLACE
				10
				1

38-39 - CUNEIFORM SCRIPT SPREAD THROUGHOUT THE NEAR EAST AND CREATED TRADITIONAL LOCAL WRITING STYLES THAT WERE SOMETIMES QUITE IMPORTANT. AN EXAMPLE IS THIS MID-III MILLENNIUM BC TABLET FROM EBLA (NATIONAL MUSEUM, ALEPPO).

39 - INSCRIPTIONS WERE CARVED NOT ONLY ON CLAY TABLETS, BUT ALSO ON PRECIOUS MATERIALS. HERE WE HAVE A GOLD INSCRIPTION (H. 3.25 INCHES/8.5 CM), WHICH IS A DEDICATION TO THE GOD SARA, DATING FROM AROUND 2400 BC (MUSÉE DU LOUVRE, PARIS).

THE PROTO-DYNASTIC PERIOD

During these thousand years the history of Mesopotamia went through alternating cycles that led to political and then cultural unity, only to turn in the other direction toward regionalism, and so forth. At the beginning of the III Millennium the so-called urban revolution had already developed. This was a historic phenomenon marking the birth of large cities that were able to gain hegemony — at least as regards power relations — over the surrounding territory. Society was organized as a pyramid hierarchy and the state was strongly centralized, with the temple and palace area controlling all activities. The model for the urban revolution rose up in southern Mesopotamia, at Uruk, and spread rapidly throughout the Near East. But it declined in equally rapid fashion. The Proto-Dynastic period I (2900–2750 BC) witnessed a decrease in population and settlements, but certainly did not mark the disappearance of the innovations achieved by the urban revolution: central power, an economy based on centralized accumulation and redistribution, the creation of labor and administration specialists, and the use of writing. The so-called Proto-Dynastic period is the most typically "Sumerian" one, and as far as political history is concerned it witnessed the first attempts to unify the Mesopotamian territory and the creation of a scale of importance and influence of the cities that was destined to last. This period is divided into three parts and can be dated approximately at 2900–2350 BC. The leading cities were Kish and Nippur to the north, and Uruk, Ur and Eridu to the south. Because of their strategic importance and the documentation they have left us, the cities of Shuruppak, Umma and Lagash should be added to the above. For a long time, the last two cities vied for control of the border territory and in their documents bequeathed us the spirit of a period (especially in its second and third phases) characterized by heated rivalry among the city-states.

The first phase of the Proto-Dynastic period seems to coincide, in traditional Sumerian mythology, with the reconstruction of the civil world after the catastrophic Deluge. The tradition of the Flood is quite widespread in many cultures throughout the world, so much so that it is thought this was a theme that was born and developed in independent fashion, but in the Near East is marked by very strong unity both in narration and tradition, so that one can reasonably conclude that it grew up in a very archaic period and then spread coherently throughout the various historic-cultural realities of Mesopotamia. Several scholars have attempted to link this tradition to archaeological finds that would prove its historic truth. The fact is, should the theme of the Deluge actually have been inspired by historic facts such as particularly disastrous floods, it would no longer refer to a single event documented by archaeology in any case, because it has by now taken on symbolic and literary features that make it absolute.

40 - THIS TERRA-COTTA MODEL (DIAMETER 24.25 INCHES/61.5 CM) SHOWS WHAT A PRIVATE HOME MUST HAVE LOOKED LIKE IN THE PROTO-DYNASTIC PERIOD. THE BUILDING CONSISTS OF AN ORTHOGONAL STRUCTURE IN THE MIDDLE OF A ROUND SPACE THAT IS MUCH MORE ANCIENT (NATIONAL MUSEUM, DAMASCUS).

41 TOP - A RECONSTRUCTION DRAWING SHOWING THE VARIOUS BUILDING PHASES OF THE TEMPLE OF ERIDU, FROM ITS FOUNDATION IN THE IV MILLENNIUM BC TO THE LATE URUK PERIOD (IV–III MILLENNIUM).

41 BOTTOM - A VIEW OF THE EXCAVATION OF ERIDU.

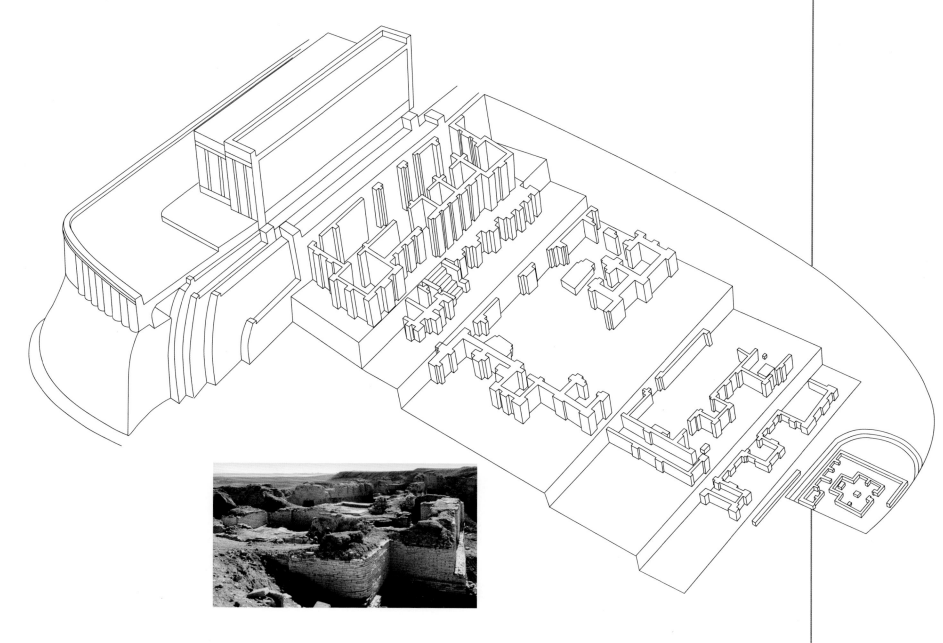

42 - Mythological scenes—with monsters, demons and fantastic animals—were often used as decorative motifs on everyday or cult objects, obviously according to the value placed on them (h. 9 inches/23 cm; Iraq Museum, Baghad).

43 left - The so-called Uruk Vase (h. 40 inches/100 cm; Late Uruk period) has several independent registers representing a votive procession for the goddess Inana (Iraq Museum, Baghdad).

43 center - This representation of a fight between a lion and a serpent (h. 5.50 inches/14.2 cm) comes from the proto-dynastic Temple of Inana at Nippur (Iraq Museum, Baghdad).

43 right - An aspect of daily life in the fields is represented in this fragment (h. 7.75 inches/20 cm) from Mari (National Museum, Damascus).

44 AND 45 - THESE TWO
PLASTER STATUETTES (H.
28.25 INCHES/72 CM AND
23.25 INCHES/59 CM) ARE
PART OF A GROUP FROM THE
TEMPLE OF ABU AT
ESHNUNNA. THE FIGURES
PROBABLY REPRESENT TWO
DIVINITIES AND ARE AN
EXAMPLE OF STATUES FOUND
IN CULT SITES (IRAQ
MUSEUM, BAGHDAD).

46 - This stone plaque (h. 10.5 inches/27 cm) has a relief with two registers. Above is a banquet scene, while below is a boat with sailors (Musée du Louvre, Paris).

46-47 - A soapstone vase (h. 4.5 inches/11.5 cm) with a scene that is difficult to interpret: a figure seated on two zebus, with water gushing from his hands. Opposite his face is the symbol of the moon and perhaps of Venus (British Museum, London).

The second phase of the Proto-Dynastic period is the one pertaining to the lives of the most important personages in Sumerian and Babylonian mythology and literature, such as Dumuzi, Gilgamesh, Etana, etc., who will be discussed below. However, a famous Sumerian text, written in the Babylonian epoch and titled *List of Sumerian Royalty*, mentions a series of antediluvian and postdiluvian dynasties, assigning to each one a period of years of supremacy in the Mesopotamian world. This text has very little historic value but is very important because it helps us to understand the ideology of royalty that developed during the course of the III Millennium BC. It relates how, immediately after the Flood, royalty descended among men, who had to share it and fight in order to obtain it. The main sense of the text is that royalty, understood as the power able to unify the Mesopotamian world, passes from dynasty to dynasty. Therefore, whoever succeeds in coming out on top thanks to the favor of the gods (or, stated more concretely, through the power of the economy or of weapons) can claim supremacy and become part of the succession of royalty. Consequently, in the Proto-Dynastic period II we can presume a certain predominance of the kings of Kish, especially in the northern region, while in the south Uruk and Ur vied for the privilege of supremacy. Bridging the transition from the second to the third phase was the rise of a sort of cult "league" that according to one tradition was promoted by the king of Kish Enmebaragesi, who built at Nippur a sanctuary dedicated to Enlil, the supreme god of the Sumerian pantheon, perhaps in an attempt to establish control over all Sumer. From Kish the king (who bore the title of *lugal*, which literally means "great man") intervened to arbitrate disputes that had arisen among the city-states. Kish was the most important in the northern part of Sumer, from where the great king Sargon hailed. Over the course of Mesopotamian history, the title "King of Kish" took on the meaning of "king of totality."

48 LEFT - THE MOST IMPORTANT RELIGIOUS CENTER IN ALMOST ALL MESOPOTAMIAN HISTORY WAS NIPPUR. HERE WE SEE THE RUINS OF A ZIGGURAT, PROBABLY IN THE SACRED DISTRICT THAT HOUSED THE EKUR, THE TEMPLE OF ENLIL.

48 RIGHT - STONE PRISMS WERE USED FOR IMPORTANT AND CELEBRATIVE INSCRIPTIONS SUCH AS IN THIS COPY OF THE SO-CALLED SUMERIAN ROYAL LIST (H. 7.75 INCHES/20 CM; ASHMOLEAN MUSEUM, OXFORD).

49 - THIS FRAGMENT OF A STATUE (H. 5.75 INCHES/14.6 CM) REPRESENTS A BEARDED MAN AND PROBABLY HAD A VOTIVE FUNCTION (BRITISH MUSEUM, LONDON).

50 LEFT - A STATUE (H. 44.75
INCHES/114 CM) PORTRAYING
KING IKU-SHAMAGAN OF MARI
(PROTO-DYNASTIC PERIOD). IN
THEIR REPRESENTATION OF
PERSONS THE SCULPTORS
FOUND DISTINGUISHING
FEATURES FOR EVERY MODEL,
SO THAT EACH PORTRAIT WAS
DIFFERENT FROM THE OTHERS
(NATIONAL MUSEUM,
DAMASCUS).

50 RIGHT - ANOTHER
PORTRAIT OF A KING OF MARI
(H. 10.5 INCHES/27.1 CM):
LAMGI MARI, WHO RULED IN
THE PROTO-DYNASTIC PERIOD
(NATIONAL MUSEUM,
ALEPPO).

51 - DURING THE PROTO-
DYNASTIC PERIOD LOWER
MESOPOTAMIA WAS
PREEMINENT IN POLITICS AND
CULTURE, BUT OTHER AREAS
SUCH AS MARI WERE NOT FAR
BEHIND, AS CAN BE SEEN IN
THIS STATUE OF A SEATED
WOMAN (H. 13.5 INCHES/
34.4 CM) WITH A VEIL AND
HEADDRESS (NATIONAL
MUSEUM, DAMASCUS).

52 - This alabaster statue (H. 10.25 inches/26 cm) from Proto-Dynastic Mari portrays a singer called Ur-Nanshe who is seated, probably during a prayer. In the development of the arts great importance was attached to music (National Museum, Damascus).

53 - A special feature of the Proto-Dynastic culture of Mari was the typical polos headdress, worn by this woman (H. 5.90 inches/15 cm; Musée du Louvre, Paris).

In the third Proto-Dynastic phase the Sumerian sources gradually stop referring to the personages of this period as protagonists of their mythology. Vice versa, there was a considerable increase in true historic documentation (epigraphic and archaeological). The first archives of clay tablets written in the Sumerian language with cuneiform script made their appearance. These were economic and "literary" records from Shuruppak (present-day Fara), Abu Salabih and Telloh (Girsu, a city in the state of Lagash). The "literary" archives contained the oldest scholastic texts concerning the Sumerian language, writing and culture. For the most part these consisted of lists of words and mythological texts.

In the third Proto-Dynastic phase the rivalry among the cities increased and many attempts were made to achieve the political unity of the area. Toward the end of Proto-Dynastic III the kings tried to accumulate royal titles in order to claim their right to control all Sumerian Mesopotamia, especially the titles of "King of Kish" *(lugal Kish)* and "King of Ur" *(lugal Ur)*. The last great king of the Proto-Dynastic age, Lugalzaggesi, the king of Umma and then of Uruk and Ur (which by then were merged) assumed the title of "King of Sumer," replacing the principle of the accumulation of city titles with the one of sovereignty based on a concept of unity in a regional territory that transcends the city level.

54 - Two "foundation nails" that were inserted in the structural parts of an edifice. The ones seen here have inscriptions by Urukagina, a ruler who promoted juridical reforms Musée du Louvre, Paris).

55 - This object is a stone head of a club probably used in cult rituals. Its provenance is uncertain; it may be from Telloh, and it is dedicated to Barakisumun. There is also the motif of the eagle clutching two lions (British Museum, London).

56 - A fragment of a plaque in relief (h. 10 inches/25 cm) with the subject of the lion-headed eagle seizing animals with its claws, which in this case are lions. This object was commissioned by Dudu, the priest of Ningirsu, who was the main god of Girsu (Telloh) and of the kingdom of Lagash (Musée du Louvre, Paris).

57 - This splendid vase made of silver plating on copper (h. 13.75 inches/35 cm) has an inscription and decorative carving. Here again is the motif of the lion-headed eagle Imdugud who is clutching two lions with his claws. The inscription is by Entemena, king of Lagash (Musée du Louvre, Paris).

58-59 - Carrying a
basket of bricks is a
highly symbolic gesture
if it is performed by a
king, such as Ur-Nina of
Lagash in this plaque
from Telloh (h. 15.25
inches/39 cm). The king is
the "servant" of the gods
and is hence the one
chosen by them to lead
the people to honor the
gods in the correct
manner (Musée du
Louvre, Paris).

59 - The scribe Dudu is
portrayed in this grey
rock statue (h. 15.75
inches/40 cm) in the
typical gesture of
folded hands. Scribes
were personages of
fundamental importance
in Mesopotamian culture
and often wielded a fair
amount of power (Iraq
Museum, Baghdad).

60 - Proto-Dynastic inscriptions are often very short, but toward the end of this period rather long ones began to appear. An example is the one on the Stele of the Vultures (h. 70 inches/ 180 cm), a detail of which, representing a phalanx, is illustrated here (Musée du Louvre, Paris).

61 - In the lower register of the front part of the Stele of the Vultures (h. 70 inches/180 cm) there is an interesting scene in which King Eannatum, who is not shown here, is making sacrifices to Ninhursag for those who died in battle and are being buried by their comrades-in-arms (Musée du Louvre, Paris).

62 AND 63 - THE STANDARD OF UR
(H. 7.75 INCHES/20 CM) COMES FROM
THE GRAVE GOODS IN THE TOMBS OF THE
"ROYAL" CEMETERY. MADE OF SHELLS AND
LAPIS LAZULI, IT HAS TWO FRONT PANELS
AND TWO SMALL SIDE PANELS MOUNTED

ON A WOODEN STRUCTURE. AT LEFT IS
THE "WAR SIDE," WITH SOLDIERS ARMED
WITH SPEARS AND A CHARIOT BEING
DRAWN BY A QUADRIGA OF ONAGERS. AT
RIGHT, ABOVE, ARE THE HERO WHO IS
KILLING A GAZELLE AND THE LION-HEADED

EAGLE ATTACKING A HUMAN-HEADED
BULL, AS WELL AS NATURALISTIC SCENES.
AT RIGHT, BELOW, ON THE "SIDE OF
PEACE," ARE REPRESENTATIONS OF
EVERDAY LIFE MARKED BY PEACE AND
WELL-BEING (BRITISH MUSEUM, LONDON).

64 LEFT - AMONG THE GRAVE GOODS FOUND IN PROTO-DYNASTIC UR THERE IS ALSO A GOODLY NUMBER OF MUSICAL INSTRUMENTS, SUCH AS THIS LYRE (H. 3.5 FT/112 CM) WITH THE HEAD OF A BEARDED BULL AND PANELS WITH SHELL AND LAPIS LAZULI INLAY (BRITISH MUSEUM, LONDON).

64 RIGHT - THIS STRINGED INSTRUMENT COMES FROM THE ROYAL CEMETERY OF PROTO-DYNASTIC UR. IT IS A SILVER LYRE (H. 41.75 INCHES/106 CM) WITH A COW'S HEAD THAT IS VERY INTERESTING BECAUSE OF ITS EXCELLENT STATE OF PRESERVATION (BRITISH MUSEUM, LONDON).

65 RIGHT - THIS GOLD HELMET (H. 9 INCHES/23 CM) WAS FOUND IN THE TOMB OF MESKALAMDUG. MADE WITH A HIGHLY REFINED EMBOSSING TECHNIQUE, IT REPRESENTS THE KING'S HAIR, WHICH DESCENDS IN CURLS ON EITHER SIDE OF HIS HEAD (IRAQ MUSEUM, BAGHDAD).

65 LEFT - AMONG THE PRECIOUS OBJECTS DISCOVERED IN THE CEMETERY OF UR WAS THIS SPLENDID GOLD DAGGER (L. 7.75 INCHES/20 CM) WITH A LAPIS LAZULI AND GOLD LEAF HANDLE. THE TOMBS ALSO YIELDED MANY WEAPONS MADE OF NON-PRECIOUS MATERIALS (IRAQ MUSEUM, BAGHDAD, NOW IN THE BRITISH MUSEUM, LONDON).

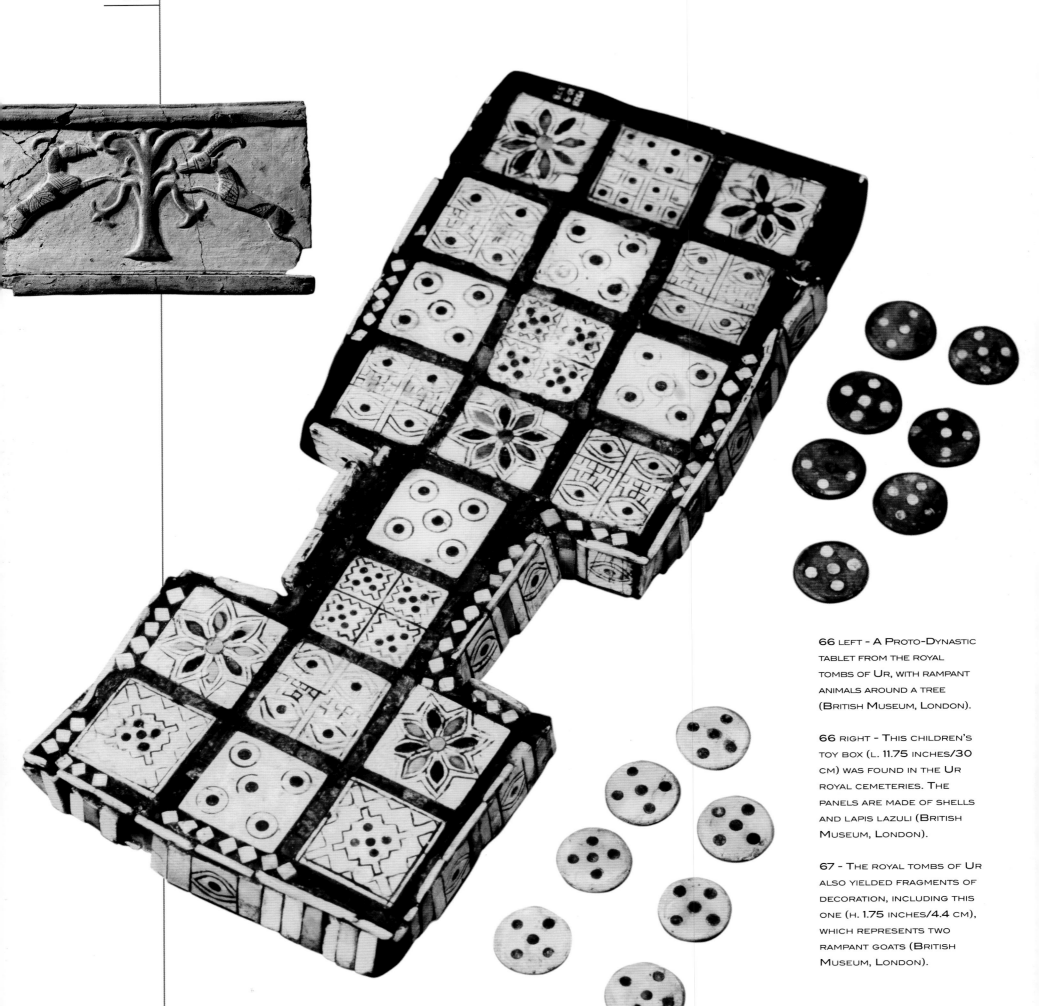

66 LEFT - A PROTO-DYNASTIC
TABLET FROM THE ROYAL
TOMBS OF UR, WITH RAMPANT
ANIMALS AROUND A TREE
(BRITISH MUSEUM, LONDON).

66 RIGHT - THIS CHILDREN'S
TOY BOX (L. 11.75 INCHES/30
CM) WAS FOUND IN THE UR
ROYAL CEMETERIES. THE
PANELS ARE MADE OF SHELLS
AND LAPIS LAZULI (BRITISH
MUSEUM, LONDON).

67 - THE ROYAL TOMBS OF UR
ALSO YIELDED FRAGMENTS OF
DECORATION, INCLUDING THIS
ONE (H. 1.75 INCHES/4.4 CM),
WHICH REPRESENTS TWO
RAMPANT GOATS (BRITISH
MUSEUM, LONDON).

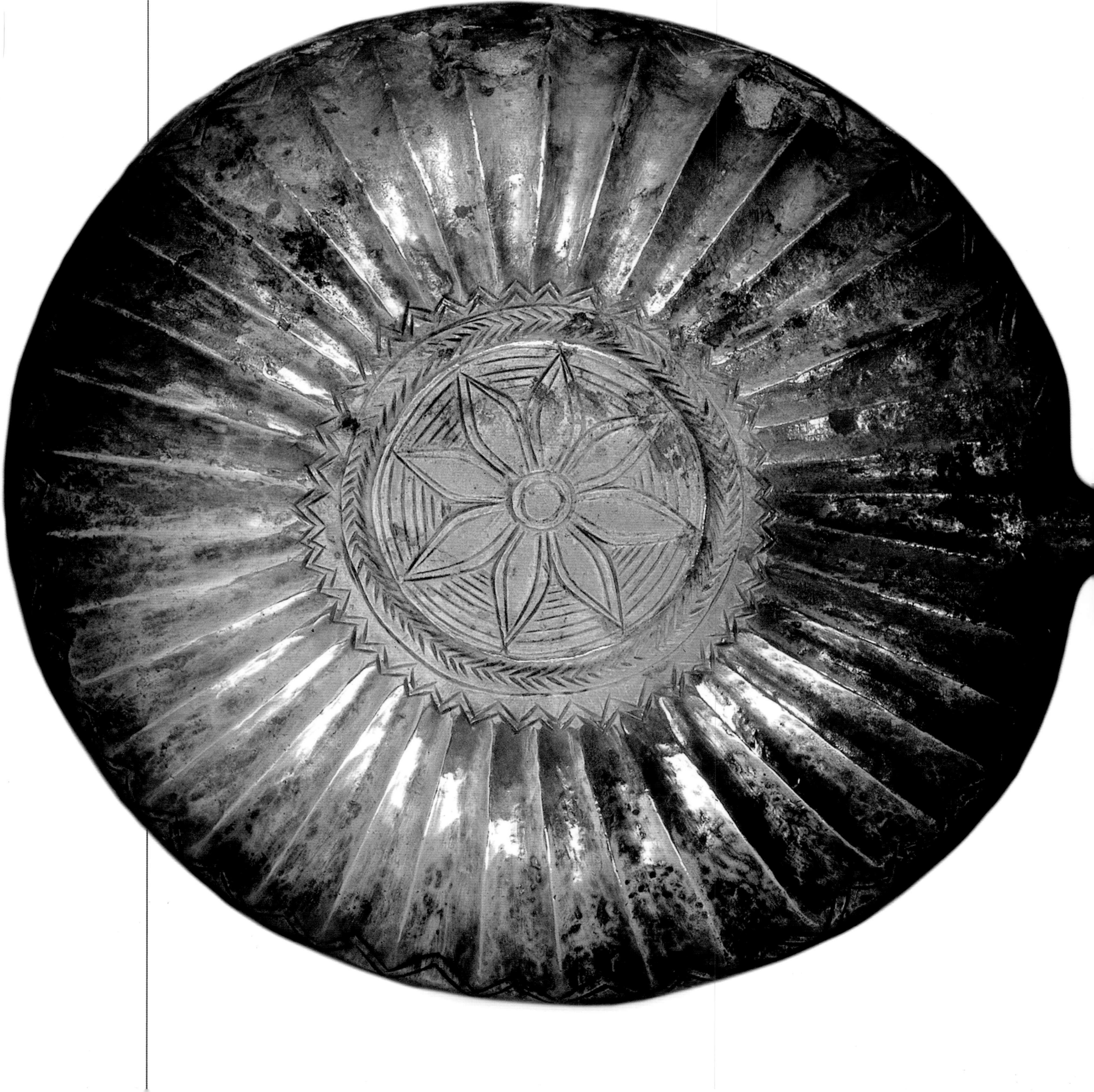

68 - This silver cup (diameter 4 inches/10.3 cm) with floral decoration engraved in concentric circles comes from the tomb of Pu-Abi in the Ur royal cemetery and is an elegant example of the precious metal tableware production of the time (British Museum, London).

69 top left - Another splendid example of the precious metal tableware found in the royal tombs of Ur is this gold cup (h. 2.75 inches/7 cm) (British Museum, London).

69 top right - This electrum receptacle (h. 3.5 inches/8.9 cm) from the royal cemetery of Ur was made in the Proto-Dynastic period (British Museum, London).

69 bottom - A strikingly beautiful gold cup (h. 4.75 inches/12.38 cm) found in the tomb of Pu-Abi has grooves and decoration on the border and a handle that turns upward (British Museum, London).

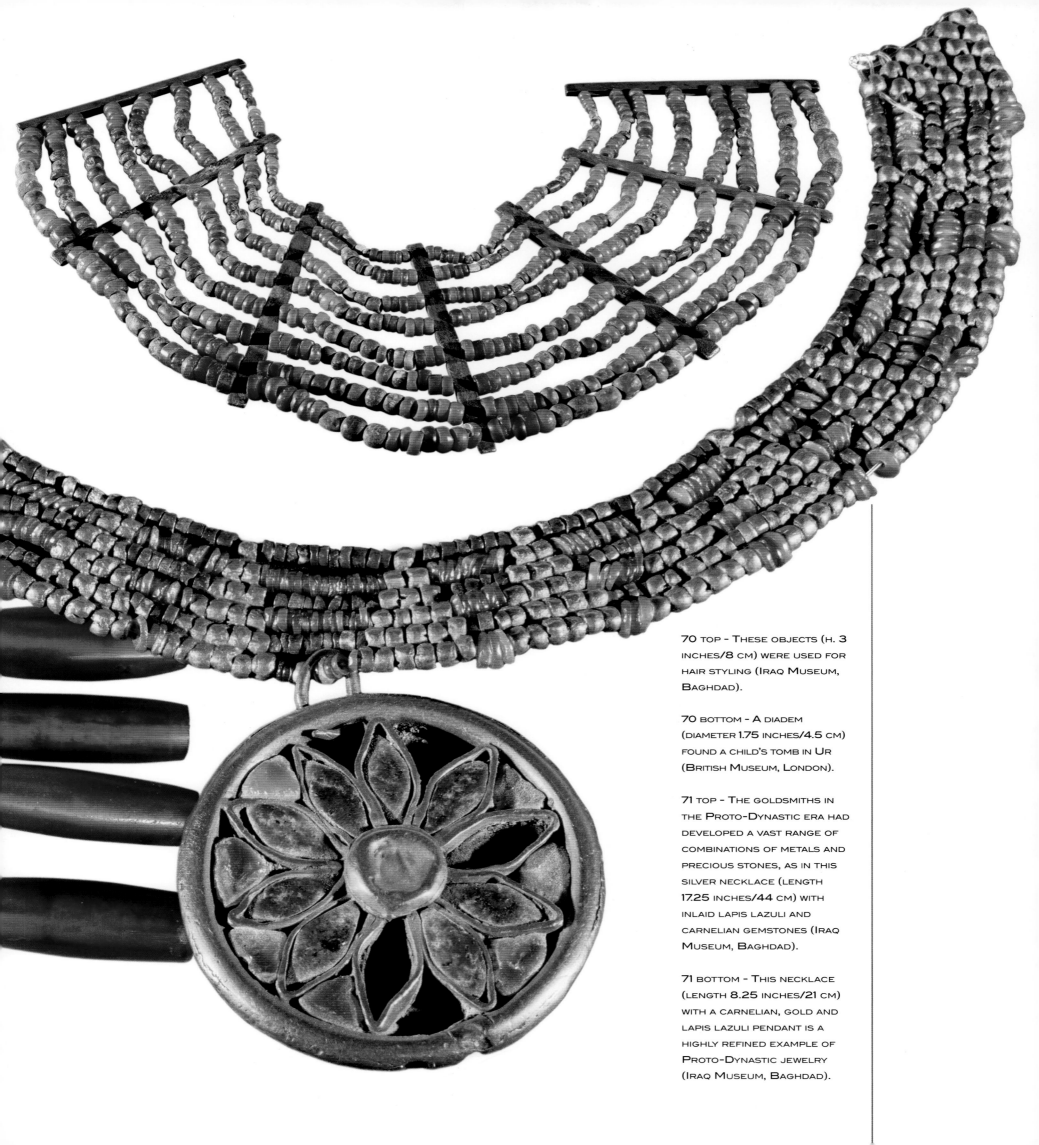

70 top - These objects (h. 3 inches/8 cm) were used for hair styling (Iraq Museum, Baghdad).

70 bottom - A diadem (diameter 1.75 inches/4.5 cm) found a child's tomb in Ur (British Museum, London).

71 top - The goldsmiths in the Proto-Dynastic era had developed a vast range of combinations of metals and precious stones, as in this silver necklace (length 17.25 inches/44 cm) with inlaid lapis lazuli and carnelian gemstones (Iraq Museum, Baghdad).

71 bottom - This necklace (length 8.25 inches/21 cm) with a carnelian, gold and lapis lazuli pendant is a highly refined example of Proto-Dynastic jewelry (Iraq Museum, Baghdad).

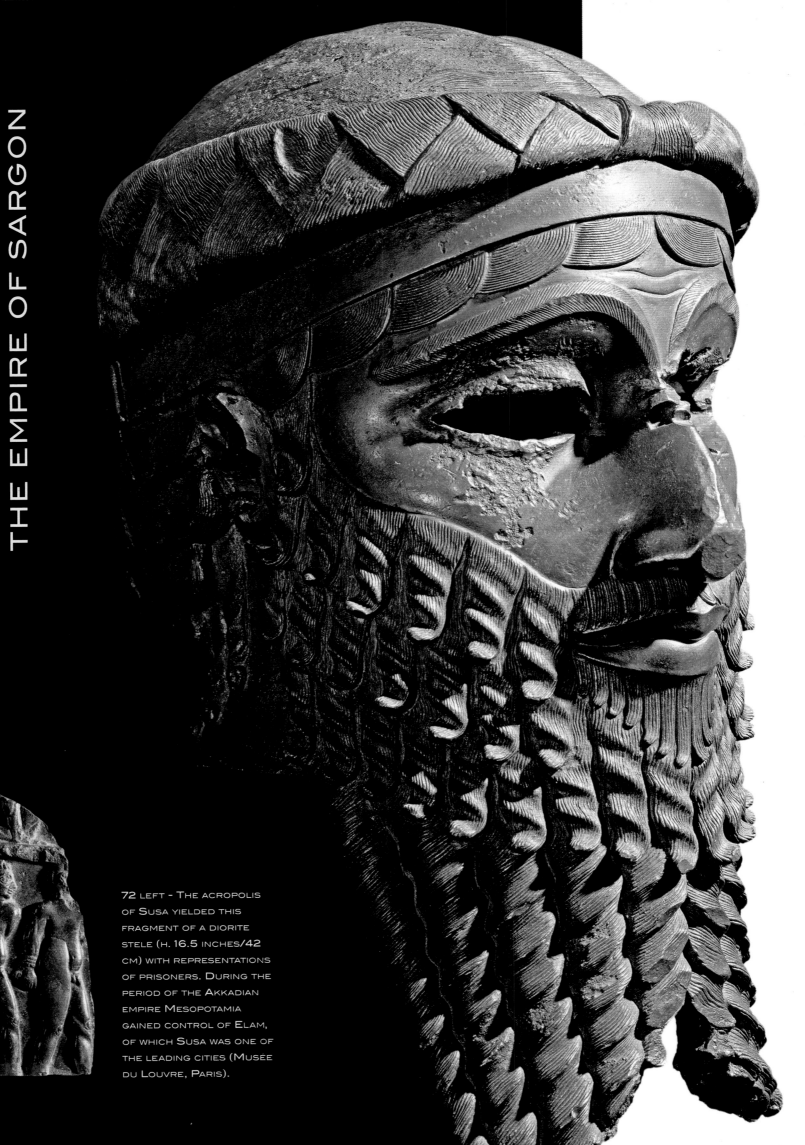

THE EMPIRE OF SARGON

72 LEFT - THE ACROPOLIS
OF SUSA YIELDED THIS
FRAGMENT OF A DIORITE
STELE (H. 16.5 INCHES/42
CM) WITH REPRESENTATIONS
OF PRISONERS. DURING THE
PERIOD OF THE AKKADIAN
EMPIRE MESOPOTAMIA
GAINED CONTROL OF ELAM,
OF WHICH SUSA WAS ONE OF
THE LEADING CITIES (MUSÉE
DU LOUVRE, PARIS).

However, Lugalzaggesi was defeated by the new king of Kish, one of the most famous personages in Mesopotamian history – Sargon. This ruler had a Semitic name, rather than a Sumerian one, which means "true king" (*Sharrukin*). Sargon founded a new capital for his kingdom, which unified Mesopotamia, and called it Akkad. His military activities, and those of his sons Rimush and Manishtushu, aimed at extending control of the land beyond the confines of Mesopotamia proper. The idea was to reach the Syrian Mediterranean coast to the west and to subjugate the Elamites beyond the Zagros Mts. to the east. The apogee of the empire of Akkad was achieved by Naram-Sin, Sargon's grandson, but with his successors this new political-territorial reality immediately showed signs of breakdown and was destroyed by its innate political instability, by the revolts of the Mesopotamian cities, and by the military incursions of the populations of the Zagros mountain range. Among these latter, the Guti were the most powerful. Their dominion over Mesopotamia was put to an end by Utu-hegal of Uruk, but it was the kings of the so-called third Ur dynasty who gained hegemony of a unified Mesopotamia.

73 RIGHT - THE NARAM-SIN STELE (H. 6.5 FT/200 CM) IS A VERY SIGNIFICANT DOCUMENT. IT PORTRAYS THE ENTHRONED KING WEARING A HORNED HAT, WHICH INDICATES HIS DIVINE NATURE, WHILE LEADING HIS ARMY TOWARD A MOUNTAIN (A SACRED SITE) SURMOUNTED BY ASTRAL SYMBOLS (MUSÉE DU LOUVRE, PARIS).

72 RIGHT - THIS HEAD OF A BEARDED MAN (H. 14 INCHES/ 36 CM) MAY REPRESENT THE MYTHICAL KING SARGON OF AKKAD AND HIS GRANDCHILD NARAM-SIN OR ANOTHER MEMBER OF THE AKKADIAN DYNASTY. IT IS AN EXCEPTIONAL PIECE BECAUSE OF THE ANATOMICAL DETAIL AND THE GREAT ATTENTION PAID TO THE RENDERING OF THE HAIRSTYLE (IRAQ MUSEUM, BAGHDAD).

73 LEFT - ON THIS FRAGMENT OF A SOAPSTONE VASE (H. 2 INCHES/5.4 CM) IS A RELIEF PORTRAIT OF A FOREIGN PRINCE WHO HAS BEEN TAKEN PRISONER. THE AKKADIAN RULERS GLORIFIED THEIR EXPLOITS AND MILITARY SUCCESSES ON VARIOUS DOCUMENTS (MUSÉE DU LOUVRE, PARIS).

74 TOP LEFT - ALREADY DURING THE AGE OF SARGON, IN THE MID-III MILLENNIUM BC, MESOPOTAMIAN ARCHITECTURE USED DETAILED GRAPHIC DESIGNS FOR THE CONSTRUCTIONS, AS CAN BE SEEN IN THIS PLAN OF A HOUSE FROM LAGASH (H. 4.25 INCHES/11 CM), WITH AN INDICATION OF THE SIZE OF THE SPACES (MUSÉE DU LOUVRE, PARIS).

74 BOTTOM LEFT - A III MILLENNIUM BC CLAY MODEL OF A TYPICAL TWO-STORY HOUSE (H. 16.5 INCHES/42 CM) FROM SELEMIYA, SYRIA (NATIONAL MUSEUM, ALEPPO).

74 RIGHT - DURING THE AKKADIAN AGE, MARI – SITUATED ON THE BORDER OF MESOPOTAMIA PROPER, JUST WITHIN THE CONFINES OF MODERN-DAY SYRIA–BECAME A MAJOR CITY. HERE WE SEE A RELIEF (H. 5.25 INCHES/13.5 CM) OF A GODDESS WEARING TYPICAL MARI CLOTHING (MUSÉE DU LOUVRE, PARIS).

75 - THIS FRAGMENT OF A STATUE OF A WOMAN (H. 8.75 INCHES/22.3 CM; CA. 2100 BC) COMES FROM NEO-SUMERIAN UMMA. THE SCULPTOR WAS RATHER CAREFUL IN HIS RENDERING OF THE VOLUMES AND THE DETAILS OF THE CLOTHING (MUSÉE DU LOUVRE, PARIS).

THE NEO-SUMERIAN KINGDOMS

The period of the empire of Akkad and of the Guti (2350–2100 BC) was therefore followed by another one known as "Ur III" or "Neo-Sumerian" (2100–2000 BC). This marked a very crucial phase in the history of the Near East because it has provided us with rich and detailed documentation, especially as regards the administration and economy. The Ur III period witnessed the introduction of some major innovations, the most important of which concerned the constitution of a provincial

system of control of the territory. The Ur III kings were among the most important in the history of Mesopotamia. Mention should be made of the founder Ur-Nammu, who built the famous ziggurat of Ur, and his successor Shulgi, powerful but at the same cultured and able to write in cuneiform script.

The fall of Ur at the hands of the Elamites marked the end of the III Millennium and of the "Sumerian" era of Mesopotamian history. Its legacy was inherited by the first Babylonian dynasty to the south and the ancient Assyrians to the north.

76 - THIS IS A TYPICAL EXAMPLE OF SCULPTURE FROM NEO-SUMERIAN LAGASH IN THE 21ST CENTURY BC. OFTEN THE KING PORTRAYED IS GUDEA, AS IN THIS CASE (H. 18 INCHES/46 CM; MUSÉE DU LOUVRE, PARIS).

76-77 - THE ZIGGURAT OF UR-NAMMU AT UR WAS PARTLY RECONSTRUCTED BY THE ARCHAEOLOGIST WHO DISOVERED UR AND ITS TREASURES, SIR CHARLES LEONARD WOOLLEY.

77 BOTTOM - AN ALABASTER STATUETTE (H. 7.5 INCHES/19 CM) OF A WOMAN, PERHAPS A PRINCESS OR A PRIESTESS, HOLDING A VASE (MUSÉE DU LOUVRE, PARIS).

78 - THIS HEAD OF A
BEARDED GOD (H. 4.25
INCHES/10.8 CM), WITH THE
HORNS TYPICAL OF PORTRAITS
OF DIVINITIES, WAS DATED AT
THE NEO-SUMERIAN PERIOD,
BUT FOR VARIOUS REASONS,
INCLUDING DIRECT
COMPARISONS MADE, IT IS NOW
CONSIDERED OLD
BABYLONIAN, DATING FROM
THE 19TH CENTURY BC
(MUSÉE DU LOUVRE, PARIS).

79 LEFT - THE WOMEN IN
KING GUDEA'S COURT WERE
OFTEN REPRESENTED BY
FINELY WROUGHT STATUES,
SUCH AS THIS "LADY WITH
A SCARF" MADE OF DIORITE
(H. 7 INCHES/17.8 CM; MUSÉE
DU LOUVRE, PARIS).

79 RIGHT - A VIEW OF THE
EXCAVATION OF TELLOH,
ANCIENT GIRSU, WHICH WAS
THE MOST IMPORTANT CITY
IN THE KINGDOM OF LAGASH.
IN FACT, TELLOH EVEN
SURPASSED THE CITY OF
LAGASH ITSELF IN POLITICAL
IMPORTANCE.

HISTORY AND TREASURES OF AN ANCIENT CIVILIZATION

THE II MILLENNIUM BC

80 LEFT - THIS STATUE MADE OF BRONZE, GOLD AND SILVER (H. 22.5 CM) WAS PROBABLY USED AS A SUPPORT FOR A VOTIVE TABLE OR ALTAR (MUSÉE DU LOUVRE, PARIS).

80-81 AND 81 TOP - A LUSTRAL BASIN (L. 88 CM) FROM TEMPLE B AT EBLA (19TH CENTURY BC) DECORATED WITH RELIEF SCULPTURE REPRESENTING LIONS AS WELL AS MILITARY AND CULT SCENES. ONE RELIEF DEPICTS THE KING TAKING PART

IN A BANQUET (NATIONAL MUSEUM, DAMASCUS).

81 BOTTOM - A CEREMONIAL SCENE DECORATES THIS LUSTRAL BASIN (H. 75 CM) FROM EBLA (NATIONAL MUSEUM, DAMASCUS).

emergence and rise of the Amorite dynasties in the traditional Mesopotamian states. The Amorites (called Martu) were groups of populations of western Semitic origin structured around a noble class and with nomadic traditions. They were present in large numbers in the Ur III kingdom and already represented a clear danger. The kings of Ur even built a wall to check their incursions into the Mesopotamian plains. However, many of the newcomers quickly adapted to, and were assimilated into, Sumerian and Akkadian society. Others never forgot their pastoral, nomadic and noble origins and were proud of them, especially those in the upper social spheres in the dynasties that took power both in Assyria and Babylonia. The most famous Amorite kings were Shamshi-Adad, the king of Assyria, and Hammurabi of Babylonia, the ruler who conceived the "code of laws" that bears his name. Thus, the political geography of the

early II Millennium BC consisted of emerging states that competed with one another and were in basic equilibrium on an interregional level. The entire Near East and part of the Middle East were involved in this process. In Babylonia (southern Mesopotamia), Isin and Larsa were side by side with old Uruk and Babylon itself, further north. Toward the east the power of Eshnunna grew, and it became the strongest rival of Hammurabi. North of Babylon, Assyria under King Shamshi-Adad was about to gain hegemony for the first time over Mesopotamia. To the northwest, Mari along the Euphrates was passing through a period of strategic centrality, a status that may have also been the cause of its downfall. From here, proceeding to the northwest, was the distant kingdom of Yamhad, whose capital was Aleppo; this was the main gateway between Mesopotamia and the Levant on the one hand and Anatolia (the Hittites) on the other. To the east, in the Middle East proper, the Elamite confederation was often involved in Mesopotamian matters.

During the final years of the Third Dynasty of Ur the phenomenon of regionalization, the disintegration of the political unity in the smaller provincial kingdoms, was quite widespread. The dispersal of power was a *fait accompli* despite the efforts made by the new rulers to claim supremacy over Mesopotamia. The first centuries of the II Millennium were also characterized by the

82 - In this terra-cotta relief (h. 3.30 inches/8.4 cm) there is a scene of everyday life in the II Millennium BC: a carpenter at work (Musée du Louvre, Paris).

83 left - This terra-cotta model of a chariot (h. 6.25 inches/16 cm), which may have been used as a votive offering, dates from the Amorite dynasty period (II Millennium BC). It is decorated with a divinity with astral symbols (Musée du Louvre, Paris).

83 right - A terra-cotta mold in the shape of a lion (h. 2.75 inches/7 cm) dating from the Amorite dynasty period that was used for cooking in the oven for the royal family (Musée du Louvre, Paris).

84 - THIS SMALL TERRA-COTTA PLAQUE (H. 4.75 INCHES/12 CM) PORTRAYS A HARP PLAYER. NOTE THE FINE DETAILS OF THIS SEVEN-STRING INSTRUMENT, WHICH WAS FOUND IN ESHNUNNA, PRESENT-DAY TELL ASMAR (MUSÉE DU LOUVRE, PARIS).

85 TOP - A SMALL TERRA-COTTA PLAQUE (H. 3 INCHES/7.5 CM) DATING FROM THE II MILLENNIUM BC; IT DEPICTS A MUSICIAN PLAYING A STRINGED INSTRUMENT (MUSÉE DU LOUVRE, PARIS).

85 BOTTOM - THIS CLAY PLAQUE (H. 4 INCHES/10.4 CM) REPRESENTS TWO MALE FIGURES WITH GROOVED, CYLINDRICAL HATS AND CURVED CANES. THIS MAY BE A SACRED DANCE (MUSÉE DU LOUVRE, PARIS).

We have seen that Mari played a fundamental strategic role in the region. The city of Mari, or better, the palace archives that were discovered there, also play a crucial historiographic role, because they provide us with a very articulated picture from both a political-social and economic-administrative standpoint. Indeed, these archives contain the most interesting documentation regarding the relations between the nomadic (or, to be more precise, semi-nomadic) tribes and the city; and the eco-

nomic documents allow us to understand and follow most of the strategic choices made by the rulers. Lastly, the diplomatic documents reveal the undercurrents of the political game played by the rival powers of the time.

The so-called age of Mari witnessed not only the clear-cut dominion of the Amorite dynasties, but also the definitive rise of Akkadian as the language of international relations that would later be adopted in Anatolia and Egypt as well.

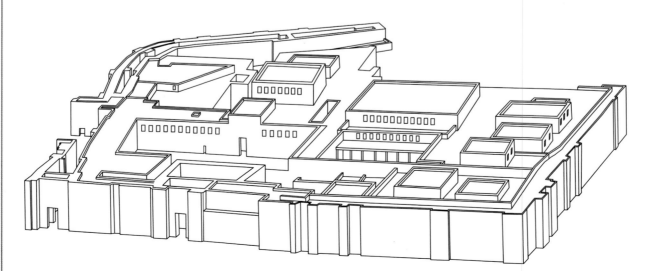

86 TOP LEFT - THE RESIDENTIAL COMPLEX OF MARI, IN SYRIA, IS A SIGNIFICANT EXAMPLE OF II MILLENNIUM BC DOMESTIC ARCHITECTURE.

86 TOP RIGHT - THESE TWO TERRA-COTTA MOLDS (DIAMETER CA. 9 INCHES/20 CM) FROM MARI DATE FROM THE EARLY II MILLENNIUM BC. BELOW IS A TOWER, WHILE ABOVE IS WHAT MIGHT BE A DANCE SCENE (MUSÉE DU LOUVRE, PARIS).

86 BOTTOM - AN AXONOMETRIC DRAWING WITH A RECONSTRUCTION OF THE PALACE OF MARI. IT WAS BASED ON A MODEL KEPT IN THE LOUVRE, PARIS.

87 - ACCORDING TO SOME SCHOLARS, THIS SPLENDID BASALT PORTRAIT (H. 5 FT/152 CM) OF ISHTUP-ILUM, KING OF MARI, SHOULD BE ANTEDATED AT THE 22ND CENTURY BC. TOGETHER WITH OTHER SIMILAR STATUES OF RULERS, IT BETRAYS AN OBVIOUS SIMILARITY TO NEO-SUMERIAN SCULPTURE (NATIONAL MUSEUM, ALEPPO).

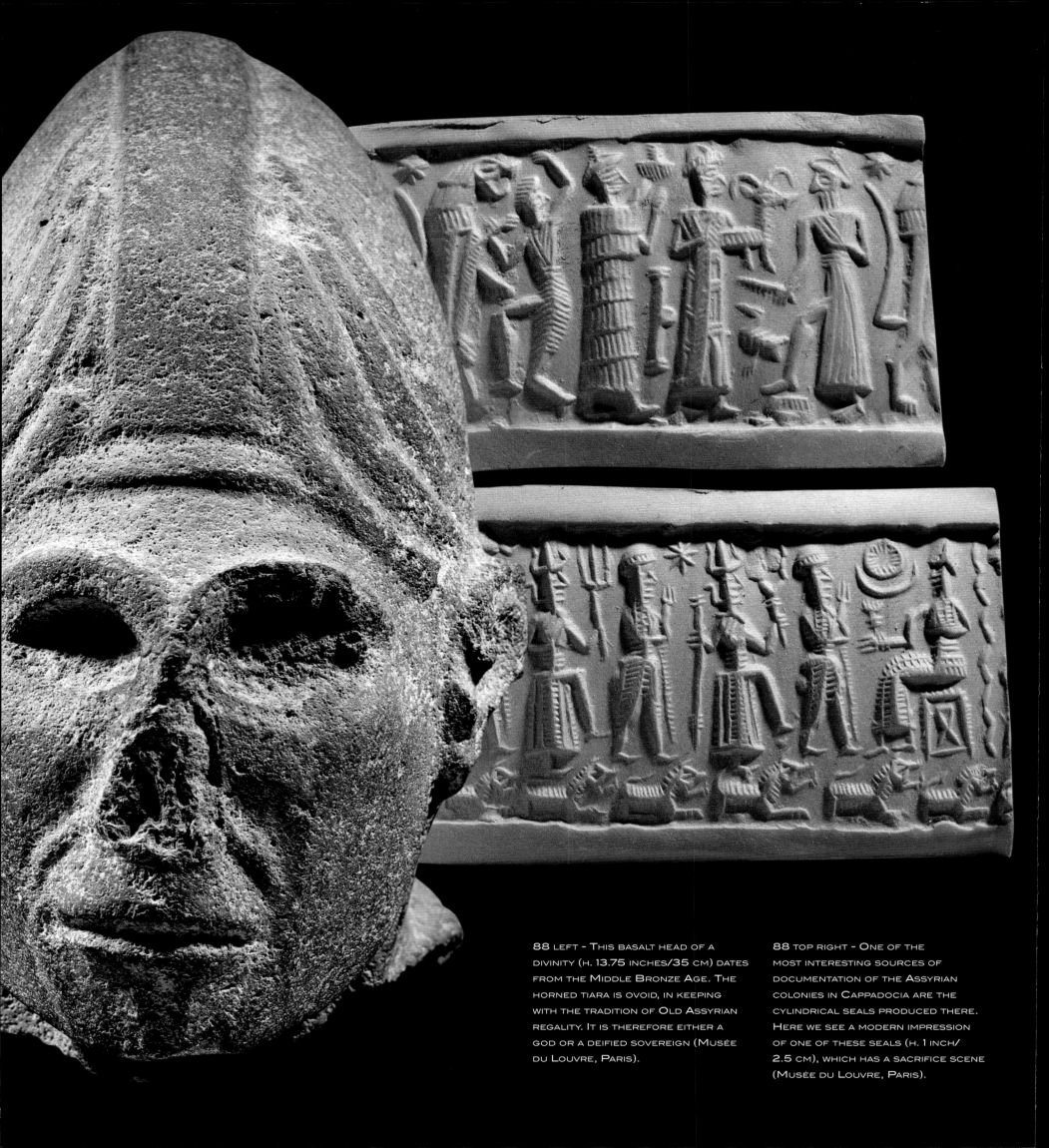

88 LEFT - THIS BASALT HEAD OF A
DIVINITY (H. 13.75 INCHES/35 CM) DATES
FROM THE MIDDLE BRONZE AGE. THE
HORNED TIARA IS OVOID, IN KEEPING
WITH THE TRADITION OF OLD ASSYRIAN
REGALITY. IT IS THEREFORE EITHER A
GOD OR A DEIFIED SOVEREIGN (MUSÉE
DU LOUVRE, PARIS).

88 TOP RIGHT - ONE OF THE
MOST INTERESTING SOURCES OF
DOCUMENTATION OF THE ASSYRIAN
COLONIES IN CAPPADOCIA ARE THE
CYLINDRICAL SEALS PRODUCED THERE.
HERE WE SEE A MODERN IMPRESSION
OF ONE OF THESE SEALS (H. 1 INCH/
2.5 CM), WHICH HAS A SACRIFICE SCENE
(MUSÉE DU LOUVRE, PARIS).

Assyria is one of the most fascinating historic realities in the Near East. It always identified itself with its chief god, after whom the capital was named: Assur. Geographically, Assyria developed along the course of the Tigris River, which from Assur (modern-day Qal'at-Sharqat) leads to Nineveh, near Mosul (al-Mawshil), and ends further north on the mountain range that now lies before the Iraqi-Turkish border. Since prehistoric times this had been an important territory as a commercial crossroad and agricultural center. In fact, the country had two souls, as it were: to the south the city of Assur was historically the commercial and administrative center, while Nineveh to the north was the capital of the "agricultural triangle." The vertex of this triangle to the south was the confluence of the Tigris and Great Zab (Zab al-Kabir), while the base to the north connects the two rivers by means of an imaginary line to the slopes of the hills. From a cultural and religious standpoint, Assur was the cult

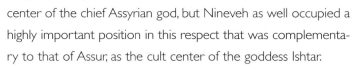

center of the chief Assyrian god, but Nineveh as well occupied a highly important position in this respect that was complementary to that of Assur, as the cult center of the goddess Ishtar.

Due to its strategic and commercial centrality, Assur acquired the leading role throughout northern Mesopotamia, partly because it had been chosen as the administrative seat by the kings of Ur, who had placed a governor (or *ensi*, according to Sumerian terminology) there. When the Ur kingdom collapsed, the governors of Assur claimed independence for both themselves and the city in a very singular fashion. In fact, the governor, who was now an independent leader, did not take on the title of king (*lugal*), but kept his former title of *ensi*; however, rather than being the ensi of the king of Ur, he declared himself the *ensi* of the god Assur. From that time, in the city of Assur the king would always be the governor on behalf of the god Assur, even when Assyria became the most powerful state in the Near East. The Assyrian rulers bore the title of king (*lugal*), since they could claim their supremacy over territories outside the traditional borders of Assyria.

However, the importance of Assur in this period was solely commercial. Old Assyrian history is characterized by great

commercial initiative that led the Assyrian merchants to travel as far away as Cappadocia and the interior of Anatolia, where they set themselves up in colonies in the most important cities of the time. Documentation of this phenomenon comes from the Anatolian sites themselves: in particular, Kültepe, ancient Kanesh, has yielded thousands of clay tablets that describe the activities of these merchants and their relations with both the Assyrian capital and the locals.

In Mesopotamia, Assur became the sorting and clearing center of the gold and silver mined in Anatolia and then transported for the most part to Babylonia and Iran. Textile products came from the south, while copper and tin arrived from Iran and the north. Furthermore, tin and fabrics were also the main export items sent to Anatolia.

The profits were considerable and the Assyrian enterprises were able to develop, but the system suffered a reverse at the end of the 19th century BC (ca. 1820–1810), when Assur was temporarily conquered by Eshnunna. The trade network resumed activity in the early 18th century, when Assyria took on a dominant role thanks to its king Shamshi-Adad. In the meantime, however, the political situation had changed, and this second period of Cappadocian colonies did not enjoy the same brilliant success. Then, when Shamshi-Adad's successors lost power, the commercial enterprises in Anatolia also died out.

Shamshi-Adad (1812–ca. 1780/76) was an Amorite ruler and built a vast kingdom that we generally consider Assyrian, since in his very own inscriptions this king bore Assyrian titles, as well as others that were more "universally" Mesopotamian, such as "king of totality." In reality, he created a huge Mesopotamian kingdom, absorbing Mari and setting up his capital in an area northwest of Assyria, at Shubat-Enlil, present-day Tell Leilan.

When, toward the mid 18th century BC (ca. 1760–50), Hammurabi of Babylonia eliminated all his rivals and succeeded in unifying southern Mesopotamia, Assyria managed to maintain its independence, but only by remaining enclosed within its traditional confines.

88 BOTTOM RIGHT AND 89 BOTTOM - A SEAL (H. 1.75 INCHES/3 CM) MADE IN THE OLD ASSYRIAN MERCHANTS' COLONIES IN CAPPADOCIA THAT REPRESENTS A DIVINITY SEATED BEFORE THREE WORSHIPPERS AND TWO MINOR DIVINITIES (MUSÉE DU LOUVRE, PARIS).

89 TOP - THE RUINS OF THE IMPOSING ZIGGURAT OF THE TEMPLE OF ASSUR DATE FROM THE OLD ASSYRIAN AGE. IN THIS PERIOD THE CITY OF ASSUR GREW IN POLITICAL IMPORTANCE, PARTLY THANKS TO THE AMORITE DYNASTY OF SHAMSHI-ADAD.

90-91 - IN THIS TYPICAL CYLINDRICAL SEAL (H. 1.25 INCHES/3 CM) FROM THE OLD ASSYRIAN COLONIES IN CAPPADOCIA THERE IS A COMPLICATED COMPOSITIONAL STRUCTURE FEATURING ANIMALS, DEMONS, MEN AND VARIOUS TYPES OF SYMBOLS (MUSÉE DU LOUVRE, PARIS).

Hammurabi (1792–1750 BC) was a true protagonist in all the sectors that concerned the authority of a king – military, political, juridical, religious and cultural. Obviously, he did not rise out of the blue, as it were. His predecessors had already directed the then obscure city of Babila to a greater destiny, laying the foundations for the reconstitution of Mesopotamian territorial unity. A short time before Hammurabi they had already attained important achievements, from a military and strategic standpoint, Rim-Sin (Lipit-Ishtar) at Larsa, further south, and in particular Shamshi-Adad in Assyria to the north. Indeed, in the early part of his long reign Hammurabi manifested due reverence to the great Amorite king of Assyria, of whom he was a faithful ally, especially against Eshnunna. When Shamshi-Adad died, new prospects opened up in the power relations among the great cities of the time, that is, Eshnunna, Babylon and Larsa. The king of the last-mentioned city was still Rim-Sin, the other great sovereign who ruled southern Mesopotamia and with whom Hammurabi remained allied. In any case, after having slowly gained land and allies at the expense of both Eshnunna and Larsa with the support of Shamshi-Adad, Hammurabi found himself in a position of power that was not yet dominant but on the other hand was not inferior to that of the other potential rivals for supremacy in the region. Indeed, Larsa and Eshnunna were considered equal to Babylonia by the king of Yamhad, who for a period had a certain degree of control over the important crossroad of Mari. But Yamhad was far away and

the king of Babylonia could initiate his diplomatic game with Mari and wait for the opportune moment to launch a rapid and decisive attack. In his 31st year of rule Hammurabi annexed Larsa and all southern Mesopotamia, and the following year he conquered Eshnunna. The elimination of his most dangerous rival, Eshnunna, allowed Hammurabi to complete his project of unification by first conquering and then destroying (respectively in the 33rd and 35th year of his reign) Mari at the border with Mesopotamia. The Babylonian king did not manage to subdue Assyria, but his hegemony was by then stable and secure. Moreover, even in distant Yamhad a gradual process of decline had set in.

Hammurabi achieved a new model of unity from a geopolitical standpoint. Initiating a resolute religious and cultural policy, he laid the foundation for a type of unification that totally eliminated the divisions of the preceding centuries. In this light, even the conquest of Mari can be interpreted as an attempt to secure the borders of a clearly defined territory which from that moment on would be known as Babylonia (but also including Sumer and Akkad). Much less comprehensible from a strategic point of view was the destruction of Mari, the major outpost along the Euphrates River. This city controlled the nomadic and pastoral populations of the Euphrates in Syria and these people would prove to be key to access into Babylonia for the Hittites of Murshilish I, who would bring the Amorite dynasty of Hammurabi to an end about 150 years later.

92 - A VOTIVE STATUETTE (H. 7.75 INCHES/19.6 CM) OF LU-NANNA IN A POSTURE OF ADORATION. THIS SCULPTURE PIECE, MADE OF BRONZE AND GOLD, WAS TRADITIONALLY CONSIDERED A PORTRAIT OF THE BABYLONIAN KING HAMMURABI, BUT IT WAS MORE PROBABLY DEDICATED TO HIM (MUSÉE DU LOUVRE, PARIS).

93 - THIS FAMOUS HEAD, WHICH TRADITION IDENTIFIES AS A PORTRAIT OF HAMMURABI (H. 6 INCHES/15 CM), COMES FROM SUSA. WHOEVER THE MODEL MAY HAVE BEEN, IT IS A MASTERPIECE OF DIORITE SCULPTURE AND MOST CERTAINLY REPRESENTS AN OLD BABYLONIAN KING (MUSÉE DU LOUVRE, PARIS).

OLD BABYLONIAN SOCIETY AND ECONOMY

Already during the reign of Hammurabi, Old Babylonian society had developed what were to be its most characteristic features. In the preceding millennium the economy had been concentrated around and controlled by the "great organizations," that is to say, the temple and the royal palace. This was a typical evolution, considering the ecological situation of the land between the Tigris and Euphrates. The productive base of Mesopotamia was agriculture, which depended on rainfall only in the area near the mountain ranges, while it was irrigational in most of the country. Maintaining and developing a system of agriculture based on irrigation meant great cost in terms of manpower (the number of persons involved in the work), intensity (the difficulty of the labor), and "timing" (most of the activities were carried out virtually at the same time in the various fields). The birth and early development of such a system required strong centralized organization, partly also to transport into the cities and towns the raw material they lacked: timber, metal, stone, etc.

The economy was clearly of the "redistributional" type, that is to say, based on the accumulation of raw material and food in the large organizations and on the distribution of these for processing and nourishment, or even as payment for the manpower. The surplus obtained was then redistributed gradually within the strongly pyramidal hierarchy, at the top of which was the king, the apex between the sphere of religion and the political sphere.

Already at the time of the Third Ur Dynasty there was a growing tendency to stipulate contracts and transactions among private citizens. This trend developed to the full in the following epoch, during the dynasties of Isin and Larsa and also during the Old Assyrian and Old Babylonian periods. There was also an increase in landed property and in the debts accrued by the small farmers and artisans. The custom of using money spread, in the form of silver weights and credit tablets, which were a sort of bank check long before its time.

Given this new situation, in which individuals had greater responsibility and independence in managing their social-economic life, there was an increase on the one hand in the expectations of attaining wealth, while on the other there arose greater contrasts concerning the legitimacy of the transactions and above all the loss of freedom because of debts. In this context the king himself personally organized the territory, for the most part by following two guidelines: seeing to the management of the construction and maintenance of irrigation canals; and assigning plots of land to officials, veterans and other beneficiaries.

The question of the irrigation canals was perhaps the most decisive one as regards the domestic policy of the country. The exploitation of the land via irrigation produced abundant and repeated harvests, but it also led to the rapid deterioration of the soil due mostly to salinization, which was caused by the lack of drainage of the salt deposited during the evaporation of the water that flooded the fields.

Certainly, the king's activities were by no means limited to the administration of the territory and the strategic decisions concerning foreign policy. Besides being the protagonist of the cultural and religious life of the kingdom, he also formulated the ideology aimed at supporting his program. The kings of the Old Babylonian period — and Hammurabi was no exception in this regard — often presented themselves as the "good shepherd," the defender of the weak, the orphans and widows. Their ascension to the throne was often accompanied by decrees announcing the remission of debts, and justice became one of the main objectives in the sovereign's thoughts and program.

Hammurabi's code of laws is an extraordinary document that describes the society of that time and also reveals some of the king's intentions and policies. This text was not the first of its kind. Already during the Sumerian era there were collections of laws, and many Amorite rulers at the beginning of the II Millennium had produced similar documents. However, Hammurabi's is certainly the most important of these codes and has come down to us in several copies, which however are incomplete. The integral and main version of Hammurabi's code is carved on a diorite stele found at Susa during the French excavations carried out in the early 20th century. On the column is a portrait of Hammurabi himself before a deity, most probably Shamash, the sun god and god of justice. The stele was presumably kept in the Temple of Shamash at Sippar, near Babylon, and was then taken away by the king of Elam as booty during one of the sacks of Babylon that took place around 1150 BC.

The text of the code has a prologue and epilogue. The prologue in particular provides us with a vast and important picture of the ideological concept of regality and of society at that time. Hammurabi declares he was chosen by the gods to rule in order to establish justice in the country. The king is presented in an extremely favorable light as the good shepherd who, despite the extensive military campaigns carried out, especially in recent years, exalts prosperity and justice rather than military glory. Babylonian dominion in Mesopotamia is presented as useful and necessary to extend and "make visible" law and justice throughout Sumer and Akkad. Thus, the formulation of the code was an integral part of the project of unification that Hammurabi pursued so patiently and persistently.

Today's scholars inform us that Hammurabi's code almost certainly had no normative value whatsoever, that is, it was not used in law courts. We know this because of the great amount of administrative and juridical texts that reveal the use of regulations that partly differ from the code itself and above all because these texts never refer to the code as an official body of laws. And in fact the cases of infractions, disputes and juridical situations analyzed in the code are by no means exhaustive and their value seems to reside more in the description made of the social order and in the exaltation of the king's works.

94 - A TYPICAL EXAMPLE OF A FOUNDATION DOCUMENT PLACED IN THE STRUCTURAL PARTS OF A BUILDING DURING ITS FOUNDATION OR ITS RESTORATION, THIS TABLET COMES FROM THE E-ZIDA, THE TEMPLE IN BORSIPPA, AND PORTRAYS HAMMURABI (MUSÉE DU LOUVRE, PARIS).

95 - THESE ILLUSTRATIONS SHOW THE BACK AND FRONT SIDES OF THE FAMOUS STELE (H. 1 INCH/2.25 M) WITH THE LAW CODES OF HAMMURABI. ABOVE IS THE KING BEFORE THE SUN GOD AND GOD OF JUSTICE. THIS MONUMENT WAS ORIGINALLY PLACED OPPOSITE THE STATUE OF THE GOD IN THE TEMPLE OF SIPPAR (MUSÉE DU LOUVRE, PARIS).

OLD BABYLONIAN AND OLD ASSYRIAN CULTURE

The consolidated unity of Mesopotamia was followed by the renewal of certain aspects of religious and cultural life. The preceding millennium had been dominated by the Sumerian pantheon. The father of all the gods was An, the sky, and his sons and the main deities in the Sumerian religion were Enlil and Enki. Enlil was the god of the air and atmospheric phenomena and of fertility connected to rain. Enki was the lord of underground waters, a more "chthonic" divinity, that is, linked more with the earth. Enlil established destiny and was the image and champion of regality. He held the title of king of kings but Enki was also very important and prestigious as the god of knowledge and guardian of the secrets of civilization. Behind these two figures lay the ancient rivalry and complementarity between the north and south of Sumer, between the tradition of the sanctuary of Nippur supported by the kings of Kish and the tradition of the sanctuary of Eridu, the very ancient seat of an antediluvian dynasty.

With the new configuration of unity that was achieved during the Old Babylonian period, the center of this unity, Babylon, elevated its own city god to the level of the apex of divine mythology, in the attempt to replace Enlil as the supreme deity. In so doing the Babylonian king and clergy probably tried to create a tradition that would sanction in a mythological context the new role assumed by Babylon as the capital of Mesopotamia. It must be stressed that the city of Hammurabi was never the main actor in the history of the country and now found itself in the position of having to share the destiny of such very ancient kingdoms as Kish, Ur and Akkad. Naturally, this process was not rapid but was part of a long-term plan that in the end produced the desired results.

Marduk, the god of Babylon, was presented as the son of Enki in order to link up again with the tradition of Eridu and to endow him with prestigious characteristics in the fields of knowledge and magic. Marduk also became the god who created the cosmos, replacing Enlil in this function in order that Babylon could gain possession of the tradition of Nippur and thus seek to achieve theological unity as well. The position as organizer of the cosmos also mirrored the king of Babylonia's new responsibilities as the guardian and guarantor of Mesopotamian order. What is more, the magical-therapeutic characteristics derived from Enki made Marduk a god "close-at-hand," who could be invoked by anyone who needed to cure an illness or find protection.

On a literary-scientific level the Old Babylonian period witnessed the strengthening of the scribes' schools, which gradually acquired the various Sumerian mythological traditions, provided translations, and taught Sumerian, which would remain the language of "high" culture throughout Mesopotamian history. The first processes of canonization of the mythology as well of other "literary" genres were initiated. The principal intention here was to place at the disposal of the scribes the various cultural traditions of the past so that new schools more in conformity with a single model could be formed.

Perhaps the most important literary work in the Old Babylonian period was the first version of the Gilgamesh epic. This great figure of Sumerian and Babylonian mythology will be discussed further on. For now we need only mention that on the basis of material now available to us, we know that it was precisely during the dynasty of Hammurabi that the sagas concerning the exploits of the king of Uruk Gilgamesh, which were written in previous centuries, were gathered together to create an epic with a coherent narrative thread.

As for Assyria, the Old Assyrian culture manifested noteworthy originality despite the strong influence of the Sumerian and Babylonian south at that time. The Assyrians adopted the terminology of the south for its own institutions, often slightly changing the meaning. Among the most fascinating aspects of this originality was the determination to assert the independence of the city at the end of the Third Ur Dynasty by proclaiming the king the god after whom the city of Assur was named. Thus, the king maintained the terminological tradition of the time of Ur, calling himself the "governor" on behalf of the god. Perhaps the sovereign, by waiving titles such as *lugal* (king) in favor of others connected to the lower administrative spheres, obtained the result of exalting the entire community, in that the power of Assur lay in the formidable commercial network it had created throughout the Middle East, including Anatolia and Iran. So the king would call himself severally governor, or prince, or simply "chief" or "superintendent" in order to attain the symbolic identification of community, city and divinity without either minimizing or exalting the role of the merchants. The traditional coronation formula was "Assur is king! ... [the name of the king] is the governor *(ensi)* of Assur." Generally the name Assur was used to indicate the god, but in the most ancient period it often indicated the city as well in writings in order to merge in symbolic fashion the community, territory and the god, thus extolling the liberty and independence of the city to the utmost. The citizens of Assur, unlike those in the other communities, referred to themselves with the formula "children of Assur," and Assur itself was more often than not indicated by the simple term "the city." According to some scholars, the word "city" also indicated the assembly of free men, thus imparting a sense of cohesion and identification that was both very strong and virtually total.

The sovereign, as the mandatary of the god, was his executor, not to mention his role as the religious, political and juridical leader of the nation. Another original Assyrian element was the calculation of years according to lists of eponyms. Besides naming the present year after himself, the so-called eponym magistrate carried out other important duties, although they are not made clear to us by the historic documentation at hand. The first phase of the II Millennium BC witnessed major innovations in this sector. But these innovations pursued, by means of different methods, a program of unity that had already characterized the III Millennium. On the other hand, the opposite tendency toward regional separateness and the plurality of experiences and cultures was dying out. The principle of unification through aggregation was replaced by the principle of the re-organization of the old traditions in line with a unitary concept guided by the new protagonists, both historical and mythological.

97 LEFT AND CENTER - TWO DIVINITIES ARE REPRESENTED ON THIS SMALL STONE SEAL (H. 2.75 INCHES/7.3 CM): A BEARDED GOD WITH A TALL HAT AND A GODDESS WITH AN ELABORATE NECKLACE (BRITISH MUSEUM, LONDON).

97 RIGHT - A LIMESTONE BUST (H. 4.5 FT/142 CM) OF THE GODDESS OF THE WATERS. THE SCULPTURE WAS ACTUALLY USED AS A FOUNTAIN, WITH WATER GUSHING FROM THE VASE (NATIONAL MUSEUM, ALEPPO).

THE END OF THE BRONZE AGE

The 16th century BC marked the beginning of the last phase of the Bronze Age, known as the Late Bronze Age. The main innovations in this period were technological and military and they also influenced the politics and ideology in Mesopotamia. The most evident innovation was the spread of the "light" war chariot, which had two spoked wheels and was drawn by a pair of horses. This chariot usually carried a charioteer and an archer. Training horses especially to draw the light chariot was something new for the Near East, where the chariots were usually drawn by donkeys, had two axles with solid wheels and were used to transport objects. The use of light chariots in military campaigns led to a veritable revolution in battle strategy, because this new weapon made it possible to launch amazingly rapid and efficient attacks. The army was therefore transformed, being divided into two different corps with different duties and prestige. There was the infantry, which was larger and consisted of common people, and the swift and deadly "chariot corps," consisting only of the richest persons, since at that time the individual soldiers had to pay for their military equipment. Attaining the skills needed to use the new types of bows (the so-called composite bows) and training the horses required a great deal of time and space, and the vital role played by the "chariot corps" favored the development of a military aristocracy that the king recompensed mainly by granting land and incomes to its members. From an ideological standpoint as well the king had to reckon with the new aristocracy and had to take on its characteristics, if possible emphasizing his status as a sovereign by bearing the best and most costly weapons and having himself portrayed by the artists in the forefront of his men, almost like a *primus inter pares*.

98 - ON THIS STELE FROM TELL AHMAR IN SYRIA IS AN EXAMPLE OF WAR CHARIOT WITH SPOKED WHEELS DRAWN BY A PAIR OF HORSES. NOTE THE EXPRESSIVE RENDERING OF THE TWO SOLDIERS (NATIONAL MUSEUM, ALEPPO).

98-99 - THE LATE BRONZE AGE WITNESSED THE INVENTION OF THE WAR CHARIOT WITH SPOKED WHEELS, A SINGLE AXLE AND A PAIR OF HORSES THAT CARRIED A CHARIOTEER AND AN ARCHER, JUST LIKE THE ONE IN THIS BRONZE RELIEF FROM THE PALACE OF SHALMANESER III AT BALAWAT (ARCHAEOLOGICAL MUSEUM, ISTANBUL).

99 TOP - THE BOTTOM OF
THIS GILDED PLATE WITH
TALL BORDERS (DIAMETER
7.5 INCHES/18.8 CM) HAS
A RELIEF REPRESENTING
A HUNTING SCENE WITH
A CHARIOT WITH SPOKED
WHEELS (MUSÉE DU
LOUVRE, PARIS).

In the Late Bronze Age the Near East witnessed the formation of some large kingdoms that divided the spheres of influence among themselves, an area where the small "vassal" kingdoms also had room to maneuver. The centers of "great regality" were Egypt, Babylonia and the state of Mitanni, which was based in the northern areas of Iraq and Syria. Babylon was under the dominion of the so-called Kassite dynasty and although it was recognized as the seat of a great kingdom it played only a minor role, while the true power and strategic center was in the border zones between Mitanni and Egypt. The 15th century represented the apogee of Mitannic and Egyptian hegemony, while in the 14th century BC the Hittite kings from Turkey replaced Mitanni by conquering most of its territory and taking control of the Syro-Palestinian zone, and even managed to wrest some small kingdoms from the Egyptian sphere of influence. The 13th and 12th centuries witnessed the new rise of Assyria and the slow decline of the Hittite kingdom. The 11th century BC marked the beginning of the Iron Age, and the collapse of the geo-political system of the Late Bronze Age. This event was caused partly by the serious political, economic and alimentary crises (for Hittites as well) and partly by the raids of the so-called Peoples of the Sea, whose ethnic and political identity is still rather wrapped in mystery.

100 - THIS SINGLE-AXLE CHARIOT (H. 6 INCHES/15 CM) WITH TWO PERSONS MAY BE A MORE ARCHAIC VERSION OF THE LATE BRONZE AGE WAR CHARIOT, OR IT MAY BE A MORE SIMPLIFIED FORM, SINCE IT HAS SOLID WHEELS (MUSÉE DU LOUVRE, PARIS).

The fall of the dynasty of Hammurabi brought about a power vacuum in Babylonia, and the Kassite kings lost no time in profiting from this situation. These rulers came from the nearby Zagros Mountains and established a long-lived dynasty. As was the case with the Indo-Aryan elites of Mitanni, the Kassites also assimilated the culture of the subdued populations without obstructing the local religious, literary, linguistic and social development already in progress. Neither the origin nor the language of the Kassites is known to us, and only traces of the latter are to be found in their names. Some scholars have formulated the hypothesis that they may also have been of Indo-Aryan origin, but the only historical material at hand is much too scarce and problematic to provide any degree of certainty in this matter.

The political history of Kassite Babylonia consisted mainly of contacts with other Near Eastern powers, especially Egypt. From the 13th century BC on it was increasingly subject to the pressure wielded by Assyria until it was finally placed under the direct control of the latter. In their relations with Egypt the Kassite rulers became famous for their craving for gold. One of the fundamental aspects of the international relations of the time was the policy of intermarriage among the ruling families. The Egyptian pharaohs always manifested aloofness in this regard; although they willingly accepted foreign princesses, they never allowed one of their daughters to marry foreigners. Thus, in order to compensate for this they had to provide large amounts of gold as a token of friendship.

The Kassite period was marked by the continuous state of crisis in Babylonia, which already during the preceding Amorite dynasty had manifested disturbing signs of decline. Many regions around the median course of the Euphrates became depopulated and the cities decreased both in number and population. Consequently, the economy favored the large estates that the king assigned to the military aristocracy and the leading court officials, and as a result more and more people fell into debt, slavery increased, and there was a prevailing pessimism that was mirrored in the literature as well.

The Kassite period was therefore a particular moment in Babylonian history. While on the one hand the unity of the country was confirmed, on the other a certain amount of political decadence had set in. However, the capital remained a rich city, not only in gold and precious goods, but above all — at least in our eyes — in culture, which became the prerogative of the scribal schools but was on the way to establishing a literary and scientific tradition that was both profound and wide-ranging.

101 - THE BLACK LIMESTONE *KUDURRU* HAD CUNEIFORM INSCRIPTIONS AND CARVED FIGURES. IN THIS DETAIL (H. 32.5 INCHES/83 CM) THE BABYLONIAN KING MELISHPAK PRESENTS HIS DAUGHTER, HOLDING A HARP, TO NANA. THE SYMBOLS OF THE SUN, MOON AND VENUS ARE ALSO ILLUSTRATED (MUSÉE DU LOUVRE, PARIS).

102 LEFT - IN THIS BLACK LIMESTONE *KUDURRU* (H. 19.5 INCHES/50 CM) THERE IS A SEATED GODDESS, WITH ASTRAL SYMBOLS AND OTHER DIVINITIES IN THE REST OF THE GROUND (MUSÉE DU LOUVRE, PARIS).

102 RIGHT - THIS *KUDURRU* (H. 26.75 INCHES/68 CM) FROM SUSA HAS, ON ITS SIDES AND BACK, THE INSCRIPTION OF THE DONATION OF KING MELISHPAK, WHILE ON THE FRONT SIDE THERE ARE SYMBOLS OF THE GODS (MUSÉE DU LOUVRE, PARIS).

103 LEFT - THIS IS THE SO-CALLED MUSICIANS' *KUDURRU* (H. 21.25 INCHES/ 54 CM). IN ITS UPPER PART ARE DIVINE SYMBOLS AND A PROCESSION OF ANIMALS AND MUSICIANS. IN THE LOWER SECTION THE COSMIC SERPENT IS COILED AROUND THE ENTIRE MONUMENT, INCLUDING THE DOME (MUSÉE DU LOUVRE, PARIS).

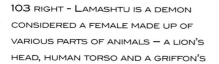

103 RIGHT - LAMASHTU IS A DEMON CONSIDERED A FEMALE MADE UP OF VARIOUS PARTS OF ANIMALS — A LION'S HEAD, HUMAN TORSO AND A GRIFFON'S CLAWS CLUTCHING SERPENTS — AND IS REPRESENTED ON A KNEELING QUADRUPED (H. 2.5 INCHES/6.3 CM; BRITISH MUSEUM, LONDON).

2

THE TRANSITION TO THE IRON AGE

BETWEEN THE BRONZE AGE AND THE IRON AGE

The 12th century BC witnessed the explosion of all the latent crises in the Near Eastern economic and political system. For reasons known to us but that we are still unable to gauge to the full, the structure of the leading states that ruled in Anatolia, Egypt, the Levant and Mesopotamia collapsed. Some large kingdoms continued to exist, but on a much smaller scale, having lost influence and territory. These were Egypt, which lost its possessions in Asia, and Babylonia and Assyria, which were reduced to their original dimensions and were for the moment incapable of exerting any sort of vigorous hegemony. The Hittite empire simply disappeared, together with other more or less important kingdoms in Syria and Palestine, in particular Ugarit.

According to reports written during the reign of the Egyptian pharaoh Ramesses III, this great Anatolian kingdom, unlike his own Egypt, could not withstand the invasion of the "Peoples of the Sea."

These "peoples" were an aggregation of populations from the Mediterranean area, whose individual origins, however, we have not yet been able to identify. Probably they included some groups from Greece, Crete, Lycia, and perhaps Sardinia. Certainly their raids could not have been the sole cause of the collapse of such a great power as the Hittite kingdom, nor does it seem probable that these peoples managed to carry out incursions into the heart of Anatolia and destroy the Hittite capital, Hattusas.

As was pointed out above, it is obvious that the social-economic system in the Late Bronze Age brought to ruin the various political systems that, after having weakened and plunged into debt considerable sectors of the people, especially the farmers, they were unable to endure the wave of famine, poverty and wars that struck the region from the 13th century on, as is attested by historic documents.

105 - A TERRA-COTTA MASK (H. 3.25 INCHES/8.3 CM) PORTAYING THE MONSTER HUBABA, THE GUARDIAN OF THE CEDAR FOREST WHO IS DEFEATED IN COMBAT BY GILGAMESH (BRITISH MUSEUM, LONDON).

106 AND 107 - THESE RELIEFS ARE IN THE TEMPLE OF RAMESSES III AT MEDINET HABU AND RELATE THE INVASIONS OF THE MYSTERIOUS "PEOPLES OF THE SEA". THE DETAIL OF THE RELIEF AT RIGHT, WHICH COMES FROM THE SOUTH TOWER OF THE TEMPLE, IS A PORTRAIT OF PRISONER BELONGING TO THE PELESET, ONE OF THE POPULATIONS COMPRISING THIS GROUP OF PEOPLES.

108 - THE STATUE OF THE KING OF ALALAH, IDRIMI (H. 41 INCHES/104 CM), WITH A HISTORICAL INSCRIPTION (EARLY LATE BRONZE AGE), WAS THROWN INTO A DITCH WHILE THE CITY WAS BEING DESTROYED DURING THE TIME OF CRISIS BETWEEN THE BRONZE AGE AND IRON AGE (BRITISH MUSEUM, LONDON).

109 - THIS SPHINX-LIKE DECORATION (H. 3 INCHES/7.9 CM) IS AN EXAMPLE OF TRADITIONAL NORTH SYRIAN IVORY WORK (NATIONAL MUSEUM, ALEPPO).

110-111 - AN IVORY RELIEF FROM A FRIEZE THAT IS A HIGHLY ELEGANT EXAMPLE OF THE IVORY WORK OF THE TIME. IT REPRESENTS TWO RAM-HEADED SPHINXES (NATIONAL MUSEUM, ALEPPO).

The transition from the Bronze Age to the Iron Age there-fore marked a moment of discontinuity, especially in the west-ern areas, but there were also many element of continuity. To the east Babylonia and Assyria survived, but without the pow-er and splendor of the previous centuries. The survival of these two states may have also depended on the fact that the ten-dency toward the creation of "noble" states had less influence here, whereas it was transforming the political reality of Ana-tolia, Syria and Palestine. Up to now, when discussing state or-ganization, reference has always been made to "territorial" sit-uations, never truly national ones. On the contrary, we have of-ten noted opposing forces and aggregations of nomadic and sedentary people, of Amorites and Mesopotamians, and the unitary kingdoms found their true "meaning" more when iden-tifying themselves with different traditions that were always competing against one another but also communicated and were capable of "transforming themselves" and integrating with one another. On the other hand, in the Iron Age, espe-cially in the western regions, the tendency to create "national" configurations was taking hold. As we have seen, the Amorite dynasties, which arrived from the west, lost their power in the entire Mesopotamian area. They were of nomadic origin, but when they penetrated Mesopotamia they soon replaced the ex-isting "urban" and territorial dynasties. This was more a change of personnel, so to speak, than of structures. At the beginning of the I Millennium, however, in the areas where the disintegration of palace and city power was taking place, the new pastoral and nomadic tribes, particularly the Aramaeans, took control of the new state organizations by imposing their own traditions and constitution. By definition nomadic tribes have a different bond with the land than urban societies. Yet the nomads in the Near East were not like those from the Asian steppes, used to a no-madic system that covered vast territories. In the Levant the pastoral tribes generally moved to the same places, depending on the needs of their livestock and their community, and always had some relationship with the cities. Having taken power in the cities, they brought a new constitutive ideology with them. The noble status of the nomads led persons to identify themselves with a group on the basis of their common origin in a ge-nealogical line, so that the members of the newly constituted states all recognized themselves as the "sons of" a common an-cestor, and the state, the "nation," was called the "House of…"

112 - In North Syria the Aramaic and Neo-Hittite states boasted some original artistic creations. This relief in black basalt depicting a four-winged demon (h. 22 inches/ 56 cm) comes from the palace of Guzana, modern-day Tell Halaf (National Museum, Aleppo).

113 - One of the original features of Syria in the period bridging the I and II Millennium BC was the use of upright slabs with reliefs, such as this basalt one with a warrior on horseback (h. 2 ft/60 cm) from the Guzana palace (British Museum, London).

As for technological and cultural innovations, there were two major developments: the large-scale processing and commercialization of iron/steel, and the spread of an alphabetic writing system.

Iron was widely used and processed also during the II Millennium, but in general this was meteoric iron or in any case iron whose processing was not yet able to produce its typical, distinctive characteristics of hardness, resistance and versatility, especially in the form of steel. In the early I Millennium BC the already sophisticated techniques adopted for tempering iron had spread rapidly and were quite suitable for family businesses. Thus, the spread of iron processing was much greater than that of bronze, which was much more difficult and was also connected to specialized centers administered by the royal palace. This is the true sense of the revolution produced by the use of iron and is the real reason why we call the I Millennium the Iron Age. Every village or even every home could have its own processing workshop without having to enter into relations with or depend upon a palace enterprise. Again, the characteristics of greater practicality, lightness, durability and hardness for tools and weapons are certainly well known.

The other great innovation, which was quite similar in some respects to the above, was the spread of alphabetic writing. The first alphabets were created in the II Millennium BC at Ugarit and Sinai. Ugaritic writing is cuneiform, while the Sinai script is pictographic and linear. This linearity probably favored the success of the second system, also because Ugaritic disappeared after the destruction of the city.

114 - AN EXAMPLE OF THE NEW ALPHABETIC WRITING SYSTEM THAT THE ARAMAEANS WERE SPREADING THROUGHOUT THE NEAR AND MIDDLE EAST IS ON THIS 7TH–6TH CENTURY BC BASALT STELE FOUND IN TELL AFIS, SYRIA (H. 17.75 INCHES/45 CM; MUSÉE DU LOUVRE, PARIS).

115 LEFT - THE SPREAD OF IRONWORK HAD A STRONG IMPACT ON THE HISTORY OF THE NEAR EAST. HERE WE SEE A CEREMONIAL AXE WITH AN IRON BLADE (L. 7.75 INCHES/19.7 CM) FROM UGARIT (NATIONAL MUSEUM, ALEPPO).

In the I Millennium the first regular alphabets were utilized by the Phoenicians and Aramaeans.

The advantages of alphabetic script were so great that it became widespread. First of all, it was easy to teach. There were very few signs that had to be memorized and they had a shape that, at least in the beginning in a more direct fashion and then later only by tradition, reminded one of a particular everyday object, for example an ox. And since the word for "ox" was pronounced *alph* or *'aleph*, the sign was read with the first sound of the word, in this case *aleph*, ['] being a consonant that in phonetics is called a glottal (glottal stop). Thus the sign *aleph* became *alpha* in ancient Greek, the first letter of the alphabet, the vowel "a." The Semitic consonant [b] derived from the word for "house," *bet* or *bait* and in Greek became *beta* [b], and so forth.

The Semitic scripts in the I Millennium were not true alphabets in the strict sense of the word, as was ancient Greek. In fact, the vowels were not written, because in Phoenician and Aramaic they did not serve to lend meaning to the written words. In the Semitic languages the vowels are useful mainly in grammar, such as in the conjugation of a verb, while the basic meanings are contained in the consonants, of which there are usually three for every word root.

This new writing system could be learned quickly, which was the main secret of its success, and it was at everyone's disposal, at least in theory. The syllabic cuneiform script of the preceding millennium were on the other hand difficult to learn and were basically the prerogative of highly specialized professionals.

115 RIGHT – THE ORIGIN OF THE ALPHABET, WHICH SPREAD IN THE I MILLENNIUM BC, IS A QUESTION THAT IS STILL BEING DEBATED AND IS SOMEWHAT OBSCURE. CERTAINLY, IN THE CITY OF UGARIT THERE WAS A FORM OF ALPHABET IN CUNEIFORM SCRIPT, SUCH AS THE ONE USED ON THIS RITUAL TABLET (NATIONAL MUSEUM, DAMASCUS).

THE MIDDLE ASSYRIAN KINGDOM: THE HARBINGER OF AN EMPIRE

In the Middle Assyrian period the kingdom of Assur dominated Mesopotamia in two different moments. The first was in the 13th century BC with the reigns of Adad-Nirari, Shalmaneser and Tukulti-Ninurta, and the second in the 11th century under Tiglathpileser.

Assyria appeared on the international scene in the Late Bronze Age, suddenly but with great determination, with King Ashur-Uballit (second half of the 14th century BC), who wrote to the Egyptian pharaoh, referring to himself as the "great king" and demanding to deal on an equal standing with the other powers, which, if on the one hand did not formally recognize Assyria as part of the group of great nations, on a pragmatic level demonstrated they knew quite well that the political-economic system of the time had acquired a new protagonist. And in fact, about thirty years after the death of Assur-Uballit, the first of the great kings of the Middle Assyrian period, Adad-Nirari, had already gained full international recognition. Despite this, his foreign policy was military for the most part, above all with respect to Upper Mesopotamia. With Adad-Nirari what remained of the old Mitanni kingdom, now called Hanigalbat, passed from the Hittite sphere of influence to that of Assyria and, with Adad-Nirari's successor, Shalmaneser, it was directly annexed. Hostility between the Hittites and Assyrians worsened

and the two kingdoms confronted each other with economic as well as military action, but the situation remained basically the same. The king who succeeded Shalmaneser, Tukulti-Ninurta, also spent the first years of his reign consolidating the frontier to the west with the Hittites and to the north with the mountain populations, after which he headed south toward Babylonia, which he conquered, becoming its king at the end of his reign.

Tukulti-Ninurta was very active in all sectors of Assyrian politics and gradually certain original features of his character manifested themselves as he detached himself from tradition. The ideology of regality found expression in the royal inscriptions, which exalted the king's architectural works and military exploits. The inscriptions in this period, such as the king's prayers to the god Assur, attained a noteworthy literary level.

The plans conceived to solve the "Babylonian question" aimed at reducing Babylonia's cultural and religious-clerical superiority by attempting to acquire elements of "high" Babylonian culture and transform them to meet the needs of the Assyrian king's policy. The scribal schools of Tukulti-Ninurta began to adopt the Babylonian dialect and it was used to compose the epic poem in which Tukulti-Ninurta himself was the protagonist of the war against the Kassite king. The great literary work commissioned by the Assyrian king is a sort of summa of Tukulti-

Ninurta's ideological program. He is the king who must fight against and defeat the traitors in order to re-establish the justice that had been betrayed by the unfaithfulness and evil of the enemies of the god Assur and hence of Assyria.

Tukulti-Ninurta was certainly an exuberant sovereign. Besides commissioning the composition of an epic poem, he had a new capital built for his kingdom, thus anticipating a typical feature of the Assyrian Empire during the I Millennium.

A violent death awaited Tukulti-Ninurta. For nearly a century the Assyrian kingdom lost its leading role in the Middle East, but it did manage to survive the crisis of the transition from the Bronze Age to the Iron Age.

After having passed through a moment of crisis during the 12th century, the Assyrian kings began to resurge and become bellicose once again. Ashur-Dan put a definitive end to the Kassite dynasty of Babylonia (1155 BC), but did not manage to gain hegemony there. Those who profited from the power vacuum left in Babylonia were the Elamites, who in the mid 12th century BC recognized that the time was favorable and took advantage of it. They devastated Babylon in several raids, and among the treasures taken as war booty were the statue of Marduk of Babylon and the stele of Hammurabi with the code of laws dedicated to the sun god Shamash.

In the last two decades of the century the kings of Isin, in southern Babylonia, took power with King Nebuchadnezzar I, but already his successors had to deal with the resurgent Assyrian power.

The long reign of Tiglathpileser (1114–1076) revived the splendor that Assyria had enjoyed under Shalmaneser and Tukulti-Ninurta, but the last great king of the Middle Assyrian period was not only a fine general. He also made a major contribution in the cultural sphere, in fact, founding a library to house the Babylonian works that had been stolen during his raid and during the conquest made by his predecessor Tukulti-Ninurta, and the style of the royal inscriptions achieved noteworthy levels. However, Tiglathpileser's power proved to be ephemeral, and for the rest of the 11th century all the Mesopotamian states went through grave demographic and economic crises.

The 10th century BC was the bleakest moment for Mesopotamia, especially Babylonia, but in the following one Assyria began to lay the foundation for the most impressive empire in the history of the Near East.

The great kings of the Middle Assyrian period between the Bronze Age and the Iron Age had in fact demonstrated that by means of an energetic, enterprising policy the nation was able to wield overwhelming and radical power.

116 - THIS 13TH-CENTURY BC ASSYRIAN STELE FROM TELL AHMAR, SYRIA BEARS THE FIGURE OF A GOD WITH FOUR WINGS (NATIONAL MUSEUM, ALEPPO).

117 - A MIDDLE ASSYRIAN ALTAR (H. 2 FT/60 CM) FROM THE TEMPLE OF ISHTAR AT ASSUR, REPRESENTING TUKULTI-NINURTA WORSHIPPING THE SYMBOL OF THE GOD NUSKU BY MEANS OF WHAT COULD BE CALLED A "CINEMATOGRAPHIC" TECHNIQUE, THAT IS, WITH THE KING DEPICTED FIRST STANDING AND THEN KNEELING (VORDERASIATISCHES MUSEUM, BERLIN).

CULTURE AND THE "STREAM OF TRADITION"

The beginning of the I Millennium BC is perhaps the best occasion to provide an overview of Assyro-Babylonian culture which, after the first phase of the revival and standardization of Old Babylonian culture, went through a second period of reorganization and canonization in the Middle Babylonian period and then began to reap the fruit of this activity, an example of which are the royal libraries founded in the Assyrian capitals. The written culture was the prerogative of the scribal schools (which were called é.dub.ba or "house [é] of the clay tablet [dub.ba]"), where the apprentices were taught not only the techniques of writing, but also a vast range of knowledge in the fields of political and religious administration. We therefore find texts that teach Akkadian and Sumerian writing, others that teach how to solve mathematical problems, diplomatic and juridical texts, treatises on medicine and divination, descriptions of rituals and other cult practices, and so forth. There are also works of "literature" such as myths, epic poems, books of wisdom, narration, royal inscriptions, etc. All this complex of texts constituted the "stream of tradition," to use the definition given by a great scholar of Mesopotamian civilization, A. Leo Oppenheim. This expression mainly indicates two typical aspects of the scholastic cultural mentality in Mesopotamia: the consciousness of the chronological profundity of the elaboration of themes, and the deep-rooted continuity with the very origins of the scribal school in the distant Sumerian epoch. In the virtually uninterrupted "stream of tradition" there are instances of conservation as well as instances of creation and/or formation, which, were always in evident contact with their origins, even if they lay at a distance of more than one thousand years. In order to learn how to write, the students had to solve a series of practical problems exemplified in the texts and faithfully copy the body of the literary texts that was considered indispensable for their training and formation. In so

doing, they had the opportunity to read and learn in depth the form and contents of the works, compare different versions, translate the ancient texts and translate them back again. In order to avoid interruptions in the courses, several copies of the same tablets were made, and in the course of time this practice brought about the proliferation of variations caused by mechanical errors in writing/copying and even intentional variations. Indeed, the sense of the perpetration of the scholastic texts did not consist merely in copying them in order to preserve and learn them. Those who pursued a "scientific" career such as that of a scribe, besides presumably becoming teachers had at certain times the possibility, or even the explicit task, of modifying, updating and saving the texts, as well as of creating new versions and even totally new texts. The production of royal inscriptions or prayers to the gods must have been an original creation, albeit deeply rooted in tradition in both form and subject matter. The case of the literary works such as epic poems, which rarely dated back to the III Millennium, was a different matter. And yet, as the history of the composition of the Gilgamesh epic so clearly demonstrates, periods in which the spirit of conservation prevailed (marked by the production of exact copies) were followed by others dominated by composition that changed the very features of the text, above all by creating a unified story from a series of distinct poems and then enhancing it with themes and different perspectives in keeping with the cultural sensibility of the time and of the people of that time.

The characters described in the Babylonian poems are the gods and heroes of Mesopotamian religion and mythology dating back as far as the Sumerian era. One of the most fascinating themes is the creation of the world and its organization. The explanations of the origin of the gods and Man and the ordering of the world vary according to the traditions from which they derived. Theogony, cosmogony and the stories of the creation of

Man are only mentioned in the prologues of texts that deal with totally different subjects. However, there are grandiose, "specialized" compositions, such as the "poem of Atrahasis" and the epic of creation with the god Marduk as protagonist. The ancients referred to these works by using the opening words of the texts as if they were the titles. Thus, the poem of Atrahasis begins *Inuma ilsh awilum* ... ("When the gods [were] men…") and was referred to as such, and the Babylonian poem of creation was and is known as *Enuma elish...* ("When on high…"). Atrahasis is not really the name of the character, as this word literally means "great sage." He is a devotee of Enki (also known as Ea), the great god of wisdom who rules over the subterranean waters, the Abzu ocean, and lives at Eridu, the most ancient seat of royalty in Sumerian mythology and a highly important cult center. There is a possibility that several persons occupied the post of "great sage." Thanks to his/their relationship with Enki, the great sage is warned by Enki that Enlil has decided to exterminate mankind soon by means of a natural catastrophe. Like Noah, Atrahasis builds an ark, putting in it everything that will serve to resurrect civilization. The poem of the "great sage" thus not only narrates the Deluge but also deals with the creation of Man. In the Mesopotamian civilizations the concept of the role of humanity in the world was pessimistic. In fact, the creation of the world had produced two "classes" of divinities, the superior ones *(Annunaki)* and the inferior ones *(Igigi)*. The opening of the *Poem of Atrahasis* describes the original condition of the Igigi, gods who had to engage in hard labor in order to support themselves and the superior gods. The Igigi had to see to all the basic operations of the Mesopotamian economy, first and foremost the cultivation of the land and the maintenance of the irrigation canals. The opening lines of the poem could not have been more essential in describing the hard lot of the subordinates, be they gods or simple mortals: "When the gods [were merely] men,

they had to bear the difficult burden of work." The meaning of this first verse has been the subject of much debate, regards the grammar of the terms used; it consists of only three words without a verb expressed explicitly: *inuma* is an Akkadian adverb that means "when," *ilsh* means "god/gods" and *awilum* stands for "man." Whatever may be the exact grammatical interpretation of the verse, there is no question as to its sheer poetic power, which is achieved by means of a noun phrase that makes a direct comparison between divinity and humanity, which immediately tells us that the difference between the two states lies not only in their condition (immortality vs. mortality), but also in their position (superior vs. inferior). The principle of a society that is based on inequality is so deep-rooted in the Mesopotamian mentality that it even spoils the happiness of the immortals. I have attempted to render the power of this phrase by translating it as "When the gods [were merely] men," in order to underscore the human condition, which, while it is not debasing (at least not for the gods) it is nonetheless irremediably inferior. One could also translate the phrase in a more simple manner: "When in the place of men there were the gods." The meaning here is that it does not matter who lives in society, but rather that this society is always divided into one part that requires the services of another, subordinate part that is condemned to hard labor in exchange for the order and prosperity of the entire civilization. The superior gods, the king, his court and retinue, and/or the elders, guarantee the order of the cycles of nature and of the social hierarchy with their power and their special condition. All the others contribute to the maintenance of their own needs and those of the more important persons. The poem continues by narrating how the lower gods complain about their sad state. They work for a thousand years, until they decide to rebel and demand that the king Enlil find a solution for their well-being.

120 - This glazed ceramic work from the Middle Assyrian period (h. 4.5 inches/11.9 cm) has the head of a woman wearing a diadem and necklace (Iraq Museum, Baghdad).

121 left - Ishtar, the goddess of love and war, is depicted here standing on a lion, the animal usually associated with her (h. 4 ft/122 cm; Musée du Louvre, Paris).

121 right - In this relief sculpture from the palace of Nebuchadnezzar II and dating from the first half of the 6th century BC, an interesting feature is the representation, at left, of Ishtar with a bow and tiara, and of Adad, the god of tempests, holding a lightning bolt (Archaeological Museum, Istanbul).

In order to allay this state of tension Enki proposes the creation of Man, who can replace the Igigi in doing the hard labor. The operation of creation is carried out by Enki and by Nintu, the midwife of the gods. In order to create the new being Enki immolates a god, Nintu, and mixes his blood with clay, so that an immortal part, the soul, exists in a perishable material. Thanks to Enki's benevolence, humanity grows and prospers, but to such a degree that its behavior disturbs the lord of the gods, Enlil. Irritating the highest god is tantamount to committing a sin, and punishment is not long in arriving. Enlil vents his rage against humans, but every time they manage to regain a state of prosperity they create the same disturbance. Enki attempts to protect humans by telling the "great sage" how to save oneself from ruin, to no avail: Enlil decides to destroy humanity and unleashes the Flood. In the history of humanity before the Flood a crucial role is played by the figure of the "great sage," with whom Enki is in constant dialog in order to save and aid men. Enki warns him of the imminent catastrophe that Enlil has decided to unleash against humans to exterminate them. Atrahasis builds an ark to save himself and many other living creatures; in the end he is even rewarded by Enlil himself, who makes him immortal. In the Sumerian poems, the great sage who survives the Flood is Ziusudra, the king of Shuruppak, the last antediluvian capital in the Sumerian Royal List. Atrahasis/Ziusudra in the epic of Gilgamesh is called Uta-Napishtim. Dismissing the poem of "creation and the Flood" as a text that is completely negative regarding the destiny of mankind would be too superficial. It contains positive notes – not only Enki's protection of Man, but also the idea that the soul of Man, which derives from the spirit of the immolated god, resists death and guarantees eternity and salvation from oblivion. The *Poem of Atrahasis* is a difficult text that has been handed down to us with many gaps that make an understanding of all the meanings arduous. Besides being profound, this work is rich in poetic images that still impress us despite their ancientness. One of the most moving moments is when the "mother" of mankind, Nintu, is horrified by the destruction of humans and curses her powerlessness, which prevents her from helping her children, who are "dying off like flies"; their bodies fill the sea just as insects fill the rivers, and they are washed lifeless onto the shore like shipwrecks. Together with An, Enlil and Enki, a fourth divinity participated in the primordial division of the universe. The four gods drew lots for the parts of the cosmos over which they would have power. An was given the heavens; Enlil became the lord of the atmosphere and of the earth, as well as king of the gods; Enki descended into the primordial ocean; and Eréshkigal became the queen of the underworld.

The protagonist of a series of adventurous, erotic poems and hymns related to cults is a divinity that was very important in Mesopotamian cults and ideology: Inana or Ishtar. As Ishtar she is one of the so-called astral divinities; she is Venus, the Semitic goddess of love and war. As Inana she is basically the Sumerian goddess of Eros, arousal and seduction, with all their overwhelming vitality.

Inana is the main character in a fascinating cycle of texts that narrate her love for Dumuzi, the king of Uruk. These compositions are truly poetic. But to characterize the intrinsic instability of the forces of which Inana is the goddess, the poems of the "descent into the underworld" and "the death of Dumuzi" reveal the most terrible side of a goddess who epitomizes a femininity that is "free" and is also the source of constant disorder. For instance, Inana decides to go to see Ereshkigal in the underworld, thinking that she will be able to return without any problem, perhaps after

having worked her influence in the reign of the dead. But the queen of the afterlife is a major divinity, one of the four that divided the world, and the harsh law that she imposes in her dominion is that whoever has any contact whatsoever with the underworld is not allowed to return. In various stages Inana is tricked into ceding the powers granted her and in the end is humiliated and held prisoner. Enki, who in some traditional myths is considered Inana's father (while in others the goddess is the daughter of An, while in the guise of an astral

divinity she is the daughter of Sin, the moon god), comes to her aid. He succeeds in having Inana freed and allowed to return to the earth, provided she send a substitute to be kept in her place. Among the various choices at her disposal she saves all her faithful servants and unmercifully condemns her beloved spouse Dumuzi.

As we have seen, the symbolic role of Inana is multi-faceted. In one myth she makes a journey to see her father Enki, from whom she obtains all the powers of civilization, but while she is on the return trip from Eridu to Uruk, of which she is the tutelary divinity, Enki realizes that, because of the beer he has drunk in abundance, he has granted her all those powers and now tries to get them back from her. Unfortunately, the conclusion of this text was not preserved, but it would seem that this narration conceals an attempt — promoted by the kings of Kish — to link the power of Uruk to the religious-cultural tradition of Eridu, perhaps in opposition to that of Nippur. But here we are dealing with pure hypothesis.

Inana and the other gods are the protagonists not only of the mythological texts but also of the prayers and hymns, for obvious reasons. We know the name of the authoress of some splendid prayers to Inana: the daughter of Sargon of Akkad, Enheduanna. This princess was named high priestess of Nanna-Súen at Ur and of An at Uruk. Enheduanna is therefore one of the most ancient poets in the history of mankind.

122 - A RELIEF (H. 19.5 INCHES/50 CM) THAT PROBABLY PORTRAYS A GODDESS OF THE UNDERWORLD AND HIGHLIGHTS CERTAIN IMPORTANT FEATURES SUCH AS THE CLAWS OF A BIRD OF PREY, THE TWO LIONS, AND THE OWLS ON THE SIDE. THE GODDESS IS HOLDING THE SYMBOLS OF JUSTICE IN HER HANDS (BRITISH MUSEUM, LONDON).

123 - THE GODDESS ISHTAR WAS KNOWN AND WORSHIPPED THROUGHOUT THE NEAR EAST, ESPECIALLY IN THE LEVANT, WHERE SHE WAS MORE COMMONLY KNOWN AS ASTARTE. THE PORTRAIT IN THIS IVORY RELIEF (H. 3 INCHES/8 CM) FROM ARSLAN TASH, ANCIENT HADATU, IN NORTH SYRIA, MAY BE OF THIS GODDESS (MUSÉE DU LOUVRE, PARIS).

Mention should be made of the other leading Mesopotamian divinities. One was the moon god, known as *Nanna* in Sumerian and *Súen* and then *Sin* in Akkadian. He always remained important, above all due to his role as the creator of time, the calendar and astrological divination. The son of Sin and Ningal was the sun god, called Utu in Sumerian and Shamash in Akkadian. Shamash acquired ever-growing importance in the history of Mesopotamian civilization, particularly beginning with the rise to power of the Amorite dynasties, which were closely bound to the astral divinities. The sun god was also the god of justice. Another extremely important god in the outlying areas of Mesopotamia was Adad, the god of the Tempest.

One of the most emblematic of the heroic human protagonists of Mesopotamian literature is Enmerkar, the king of the first dynasty of Uruk, who deserves the great honor of having invented writing. In the poems in which he is the main character, Enmerkar confronts the king of Aratta, a city (Elamite?) on the Iranian plateau. There were complex economic and political relations between Uruk and Aratta that also involved the problem of the supremacy decreed by Inana. Both rulers believed they were the favorites of Inana, but Enmerkar, by inventing the art of writing, presented it with great pride as a sign of superiority and divine favor.

124 LEFT - THE GOD OF TEMPESTS IS PORTRAYED IN THIS STELE FROM ASSUR (H. 4.5 FT/1.36 M) WHILE HE IS WALKING ON A BULL, THE ANIMAL THAT IS HIS SYMBOL (MUSÉE DU LOUVRE, PARIS).

124 RIGHT - THE MOON GOD IS DEPICTED ON AN 8TH-CENTURY BC STELE FROM TELL AHMAR AMONG THE TYPICAL SYMBOLS OF THE CRESCENT MOON (NATIONAL MUSEUM, ALEPPO).

125 - A REPRESENTATION OF ADAD AND ISHTAR FROM THE ARAMAIC KINGDOM OF GUZANA (TELL HALAF), DATING FROM THE 9TH CENTURY BC (NATIONAL MUSEUM, ALEPPO).

Lastly, we shall now turn to the greatest and most important literary work in all Mesopotamian culture, the *Gilgamesh Epic*. Many intellectuals participated in the creation of this work, both as bearers of original contributions and as compilers and editors of preceding traditions. The classic text consists of twelve tablets written in Akkadian, compiled in the Neo-Assyrian period but probably dating to the Middle Babylonian period, that is, around the 12th century BC. The first attempt made at writing a unitary composition is even more ancient, dating from the Old Babylonian period, but only a few fragments of this version have survived. The idea that in the Old Babylonian period there existed an already consolidated unitary tradition around a text considered a cornerstone of crucial importance and value is confirmed by the diffusion that the stories of the king of Uruk Gilgamesh enjoyed in the entire Near East, up to Elam and Anatolia, among the Hittites. Gilgamesh is also mentioned in ancient Greek texts, in the writings on Babylonian civilization by Berossus.

The epic poem of Gilgamesh is also the longest in all Babylonian literature.

The protagonist is a king of Uruk, "two-thirds god and one-third human," as the prologue tells us. The distinguishing features of this personage, which are so well described that they make him a universal literary symbol, are connected to his awareness and knowledge of the mysteries of life and death. Although he is mostly divine, our hero is condemned to share the lot of all other human beings — death. His thirst for knowledge and immortality lead him to, and inspire him in, his various feats, particularly the last one, the journey in search of Uta-Napishtim, the great ancient sage chosen to save humanity after the catastrophic Flood. Uta-Napishtim reveals the secret of the eternal youth of the gods to Gilgamesh: a plant, the tree of life. The old man makes a gift of it to Gilgamesh, who unfortunately loses it forever, for while he is bathing a serpent eats it (tablet XI). Before his desperate quest for immortality, the king of Uruk performs feats that are grandiose and, because of his craving after grandeur, irreverent. Indeed, he challenges no less a divinity than the goddess Inana, repudiating her love and killing the Celestial Bull, which is sacred to the goddess and has been sent to destroy Uruk. But in reality Gilgamesh's power is also due to a faithful ally, his dear friend Enkidu, created deliberately as a counter to the bellicose king who sent his soldiers to the front, leaving their poor fiancées all alone. But whereas Enkidu manages to inject a certain measure of equilibrium in Gilgamesh's soul, he certainly does not diminish the king's desire to perform great feats. The first of these is the conquest of the cedar forest, guarded by the monster Humbaba, and the second the already mentioned slaying of the Celestial Bull. At the peak of his glory, accompanied by his beloved friend, Gilgamesh certainly does not expect this imminent tragedy. The sins of hubris committed by the two had to be punished with the death of one of them: Enkidu. The feeling of impotence when faced with the death of his friend arouses in the king the imperative need to gain knowledge of eternal life. In a limited amount of space, it is by no means easy to discuss such an important work in the history of the human spirit, but on the other hand, dealing in depth with the themes and problems it involves would require an entire treatise.

The body of Mesopotamian literary texts also includes treatises on magic, divination, medicine and mathematics. In this regard, particular mention should be made of the "lists." The Sumerians and Babylonians catalogued all the knowledge of the time in the form of tables, which included dictionaries and handbooks to help readers understand the Sumerian ideograms. An important part of this body of "encyclopedic lists" consisted of treatises containing various types of mantic or oracular responses.

The art of interpreting the signs that the gods left in the world of the senses was quite deeply rooted in Mesopotamian culture. Mantic is the science of divination, of the interpretation of presages, which may be of two types, either "spontaneous" or "provoked." Thus, the diviner had to specialize in one of the many techniques of "asking" the gods for presages or of "discovering" spontaneously consigned messages. In any case, the main task in every situation was interpretation. Over the centuries the scribal school furnished lists of typical phenomena for the various divinatory sciences, together with the relevant interpretations, always attempting to canonize a system of thought in an increasingly thorough and totalizing manner.

The most important divinatory arts were lecanomancy (the inspection of oil in water), libanomancy (the observation of incense smoke), hepatoscopy (the inspection of the liver, practiced especially during the Old Babylonian dynasty), extispicy (the inspection of entrails), and astrology. While it is true that divination in itself was one of the most characteristic features of all Mesopotamian cultures, it took on different forms and utilized different methods, thus creating a highly stratified history in the various periods and regions. Astrology, which began to spread and take on importance during the Kassite epoch, attained its apogee at the court of the Neo-Assyrian and Neo-Babylonian kings and remained important up to the age of Seleucid dominion.

126 - THIS RELIEF (H. 14.5 FT/4.45 M) FROM THE PALACE OF SARGON II REPRESENTS A PROTECTIVE GENIE TRANSPORTING A SMALL LION. IN THE PAST IT WAS THOUGHT TO BE A REPRESENTATION OF GILGAMESH (MUSÉE DU LOUVRE, PARIS).

127 - THE STORIES CONNECTED TO GILGAMESH WERE VERY WIDESPREAD AS ICONOGRAPHIC MOTIFS. THIS RELIEF (H. 5 INCHES/13 CM) EXECUTED IN THE FIRST HALF OF THE II MILLENNIUM BC DEPICTS THE HERO KILLING THE MONSTER HUBABA (VORDERASIATISCHES MUSEUM, BERLIN).

3

THE GREAT ASSYRIAN EMPIRE

THE BIRTH AND INITIAL EXPANSION OF THE NEO-ASSYRIAN KINGDOM

It took about two centuries for Assyria – reduced to its original nucleus but well aware that it was in a position to consider at the very least all Upper Mesopotamia as its natural territorial borders – to take into hand the political, economic, military and cultural situation in the Near East. In fact, this time the kings of Assur set about gaining control of the entire Near East, including Anatolia, Egypt and Iran.

In the I Millennium, given the technological innovations and the capacity to use and distribute them, and the new social realities and ideologies mentioned in the preceding chapter, the geopolitical sphere was subject to new conditions and possibilities.

There was a great and rapid increase in the range of the physical (as well as psychological and ideological) space within which the great powers operated. In other words, what occurred was that, in the same territory (Mesopotamia, for example) there was a drastic reduction in the density of the cities or states capable of imposing their influence, be it political, economic or cultural, so that it was now possible for a single state to exist in what a few centuries earlier had been vast areas dotted with several rival kingdoms. This emerging power was bordered by other powers that, in order to be so well developed, had also had the possibility of gaining access to a large quantity of demographic and physical resources. The level of organicity and compactness of the large state organizations was becoming increasingly uniform in a world in which a certain degree of equilibrium was achieved partly because of the

distance between the centers of the new powers, which was now much greater than before. Indeed, in the second half of the millennium Mesopotamia became a small, albeit significant, part of an imperial complex with a network of direct contacts due to dominion or alliances that would have seemed incommensurable in the eyes of the typical geographic mentality of Mesopotamian culture in the II Millennium. In fact, the Persian Empire would be the new center of a map of the Earth that extended from the Indian subcontinent to the Iberian Peninsula, from the Himalayas to the Strait of Gibraltar.

Technological innovations contributed quite a lot to this change in the use and perception of the land. The processing of iron as the basic metal for making everyday and work tools facilitated the widespread distribution of towns and cities, but also triggered significant progress in the field of civil and military engineering. The Iron Age witnessed the development of a series of techniques for land improvement that led to its being transformed and adapted in an even more radical and extensive manner than before. For example, large areas of terracing were created, thus making intensive cultivation possible even in hilly and foothill areas. The means of transport were improved, especially ships, and there was a growing tendency to have smaller but more widespread cities. In short, in the I Millennium both human society and the environment were gradually taking on a more and more "modern" configuration and aspect.

128 - DETAIL OF A RELIEF OF ASSURNASIRPAL II AT NIMRUD (BRITISH MUSEUM, LONDON).

130 LEFT - A BRONZE QUIVER (H. 2 FT/61 CM) WITH FIVE STORIED REGISTERS (MUSÉE DU LOUVRE, PARIS).

130 RIGHT - THIS EMBOSSED BRONZE FRAGMENT FROM BALAWAT MUST HAVE BEEN PART OF THE PLATING OF A CITY GATE (ARCHAEOLOGICAL MUSEUM, ISTANBUL).

131 - A FRAGMENT OF A RELIEF SCULPTURE (H. 9.5 INCHES/24 CM) FROM DUR-SHARRUKIN (KHORSABAD) PORTRAYING A BEARDED MAN WITH A HEADDRESS (MUSÉE DU LOUVRE, PARIS).

Assyria was one of the first states to exploit the new potential offered in this millennium, above all in a political key. At first it did so perhaps in a less conscious fashion, through acts aimed basically at reviving what in the Late Bronze Age the kings referred to as the country of Assur. But at a later stage this became a sudden and determined move toward the realization of a territorial state that was both the only one of its kind and unitary, that is, culturally structured so that everything would be in relation with the center (the original nucleus of Assur), which was achieved by "Assyrianizing" Mesopotamia and the territories traditionally connected to it.

Thus, in the first phase Assyria took back the land that it considered an integral part of the nation at the time of Tukulti-Ninurta I, and then consolidated the frontiers. The army also served to guarantee the payment of tributes on the part of vassal states.

The history of this early stage was marked mostly by the military campaigns waged on the three major fronts by the Assyrian kings. To the north were the regions of the Tigris River basin and its left-hand affluents, which even penetrated the Armenian Taurus Mts. and the Zagros Mts. in northwestern Iran. Key areas were Lake Urmia and Lake Van, which were controlled by a coalition of Urartian people that called itself Nairi. And very soon Nairi became a unified nation known as Urartu.

132 - A THEME TYPICAL OF URARTIAN CULTURE (ARMENIA) IS ON THIS 8TH–7TH CENTURY BRONZE PLAQUE (H. 5.5 INCHES/ 13.8 CM): A DIVINITY IS TREADING ON A LION IN FRONT OF A WORSHIPPER (MUSÉE DU LOUVRE, PARIS)

133 - THIS BRONZE STATUETTE OF THE DEMON PAZUZU (H. 6 INCHES/15 CM) WAS FOUND IN TELL SHEIKH AHMED, SYRIA AND DATES FROM THE 7TH CENTURY BC. THE DEMON HAD THE POWER TO DRIVE AWAY EVIL SPIRITS AND ILLNESS (MUSEUM OF DEIR-EZ-ZOR).

The western front included the Aramaic states in "Middle Assyrian" territory, between Habur and Balih, and those more to the west, along and beyond the Euphrates River. This front was extended by Tiglathpileser III to Palestine and the median course of the Euphrates. The southern front mainly consisted of Babylonia and the Chaldaean tribes that had settled in the south of the country along the Persian Gulf and several times had attempted to conquer Babylon itself.

Thus, at the end of the 10th century BC Adad-nirari II and Tukulti-Nirnurta II (911–891 and 890–884 BC respectively) regained and consolidated the interior borders, an area that was more or less the same as that ruled by Tukulti-Ninurta I in the Late Bronze Age. The main objective was to control the most important trade routes to the Mediterranean and Anatolia, and also drive out the Armenians who had infiltrated Assyrian territory and colonized the zone again. Assurnasirpal II (883–859) began to take his army beyond the traditional borders, but he was important historically mainly for the construction works he promoted in person. He built the new capital, Calah (Kalakh), with the so-called Northwest Palace, which was decorated with cycles of impressive and hieratic bas-reliefs and

sculptures. During the reign of Assurnasirpal II, to the north the new kingdom of Urartu was being formed, and it was immediately confronted by Shalmaneser III (858–824), whose reign was distinguished by the intensification of military campaigns on all the fronts, including the southern one.

During the reign of the successive kings, from Shamshi-Adad V to Assur-nirari V, Assyria went through a period of domestic crisis under the shadow of such gray eminences as Queen Semiramis and the turtanu (supreme commander) Shamshi-ilu.

Around the mid-8th century BC this crisis actually undermined Assyrian supremacy. Sarduri of Urartu became the leader of the anti-Assyrian Neo-Hittite coalition, but in 744 BC Tiglathpileser III took power, effecting drastic innovations and achieving significant military victories. In 743 he won the battle of Kishtan against Sarduri and the Neo-Hittite states, whereupon he immediately embarked on a policy of permanent conquest by means of a provincial system, but first concentrating on Palestine. His successor Shalmaneser V (726–722 BC) introduced some major administrative innovations, first abolishing the old privileges held by the holy cities of Assur and Harran (the cult center of the moon god and the third-ranking religious center of the Neo-Assyrian kingdom after Assur and Nineveh). A revolt broke out and Sargon II (721–705 BC) took power.

137 - Very little of Assyrian painting has been preserved. In this example from Nimrud (h. 11 inches/30 cm) a king, perhaps Assurnasirpal II, is accompanied by his retinue. A widely used pictorial medium was glazed clay, whose colors were limited to the essential (British Museum, London).

136 top - The powerful king Assurnasirpal II gathered booty and tributes from everywhere and placed them in his palace in Kalakh (Nimrud). The metalware found there has decoration with motifs from various sources. This piece (diameter 8.5 inches/22 cm) is made of bronze (British Museum, London).

136 bottom - This precious object (diameter 8.5 inches/21.7 cm) was also probably a part of tributes or war booty. Its decoration reminds one of Phoenician production (British Museum, London).

138 - AN IVORY PLAQUE (H. 10 INCHES/25.5 CM) WITH A MAN HOLDING A PALM UNDER A WINGED SYMBOL (IRAQ MUSEUM, BAGHDAD).

139 - THIS IVORY PLAQUE FROM NIMRUD (H. 6.5 INCHES/16.8 CM) IS KNOWN AS "MONA LISA" (IRAQ MUSEUM, BAGHDAD).

140 - A MARVELOUS LION'S HEAD MADE OF IVORY (H. 2 INCHES/5.5 CM) FOUND AT FORT SALMANESER, AT NIMRUD (ANCIENT KALAKH), WHICH BECAME THE NEO-ASSYRIAN CAPITAL UNDER ASSURNASIRPAL II (BRITISH MUSEUM, LONDON).

141 - THIS SPLENDID EXAMPLE OF THE IVORY WORK FOUND AT NIMRUD (H. 2.75 INCHES/6.9 CM) IN THE AREA KNOWN AS FORT SALMANESER REPRESENTS A SPHINX WALKING AMONG PLANT MOTIFS (BRITISH MUSEUM, LONDON).

142 AND 143 - THE BASALT BLACK OBELISK OF SALMANESER III (H. 6.5 FT/200 CM; SECOND HALF OF THE 9TH CENTURY BC) NARRATES VARIOUS EPISODES OF THE KING'S REIGN. HERE WE SEE KING JEHU OF ISRAEL SUBMITTING TO SALMANESER III (P. 142 BELOW AND 142-143) AND ROWS OF TRIBUTARIES BEARING GIFTS TO HIM (P. 143) (BRITISH MUSEUM, LONDON).

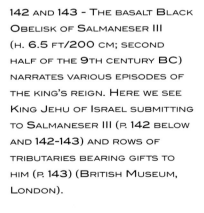

144-145 - This enlargement of one of the panels in the Black Obelisk of Salmaneser III shows some figures transporting gifts for the king. In the middle and at right there may be objects that were also used for cult rituals (British Museum, London).

146 AND 147 - THE EMBOSSED BRONZE
RELIEFS OF THE GATES OF BALAWAT IN
THE PALACE OF SALMANESER III (SECOND
HALF OF THE 9TH CENTURY BC)
NARRATE SCENES OF VARIOUS KINDS:
ROWS OF BEARERS, SOME OF WHOM ARE
LEAVING FROM A PORT (P. 146 ABOVE
AND CENTER; H. 3.25 INCHES/8.5 CM);
KING SALMANESER III GREETING
FOREIGN TRIBUTARIES (P. 146 BELOW; H.
5 INCHES/12.5 CM); AND BATTLE SCENES
ON SEVERAL SUPERPOSED REGISTERS (P.
147; H. 6.25 INCHES/16 CM) (MUSÉE DU
LOUVRE, PARIS).

148 - The provincial palace of Til Barsip, conquered by Salmaneser III in 856 BC, is decorated with fresco cycles. This fragment (H. 12 inches/ 30.7 cm), which may be a portrait of a tributary of the king, is a fine example of Assyrian painting, very little of which has been preserved (Musée du Louvre, Paris).

149 - A magnificent fresco fragment (H. 16 inches/40.5 cm) from the provincial palace of Til Barsip that most probably depicts two Assyrian dignitaries. Part of the original color has been preserved (National Museum, Aleppo).

150 TOP LEFT - THIS FRAGMENT OF A RELIEF (H.7 FT/ 211 CM) FROM NIMRUD HAS A BATTLE SCENE WITH KING TIGLATHPILESER III (BRITISH MUSEUM, LONDON).

150 TOP RIGHT - A RELIEF FOUND IN NIMRUD (H. 3.25 FT/99 CM) OF A CITY FORTIFICATION THAT TIGLATHPILESER III ENCOUNTERED DURING HIS MILITARY CAMPAIGNS IN THE NORTH (MUSÉE DU LOUVRE, PARIS).

150 BOTTOM - SOLDIERS WITH MACES ARE ILLUSTRATED IN THIS DETAIL OF A RELIEF FROM ARSLAN TASH (ARCHAEOLOGICAL MUSEUM, ISTANBUL).

151 - IN THIS RELIEF (H. 7 FT/211 CM), WHICH MAY NARRATE THE BATTLE OF TIGLATPILESER III AGAINST UPA (ANATOLIA?), THERE ARE WOUNDED ARCHERS ON THE GROUND, A WAR MACHINE FOR SIEGES, AND SOME MEN BEING SENT TO THE GALLOWS (BRITISH MUSEUM, LONDON).

THE PROGRAM OF CONQUEST AND DOMINION

When Sargon II ascended the throne in 721 BC Assyria had already become a firmly entrenched large empire. It had passed through a serious domestic crisis caused by the fact that the administrative structures had proved to be incapable of dealing with the new political reality and the great power that some figures of the court – either generals or royal family members – had acquired. Once the crisis had been overcome, thanks to Tiglathpileser III's vigorous policy, the new king Sargon II first had to face the problem of rewarding those who had supported him in the rebellion against the awkward and unconventional ruler Salmanassar V, soon afterward embarking on his projects of expansion of the country, which was understood as a political organism and not only as mere territory on which one had the right to exact tribute. Sargon II began the period of greatest splendor for Assyrian civilization by participating in person and with great determination in all areas of royal activity. He made the most extensive conquests of all the Assyrian kings: the Neo-Hittite kingdoms between Syria and Turkey, Cyprus, most of the Syro-Palestinian states that had managed to remain independent after the wars waged by Tiglathpileser III, the Chaldaean tribes, and the entire border zone toward the Zagros and Taurus Mts. These military campaigns were flanked by dedication to the reorganization and centralization of the empire administration, which came about partly because of a great deal of imposed deportation and colonization. But the main reason for the present-day fame of Sargon II lies in the grandiose construction of the new capital Dur Sharrukin, an enormous construction site that bore the name of the king (*Sharru-kin*, or "true king," like the mythical Sargon of Akkad) and that expressed the king's desire for order through buildings laid out on a grid plan and decorated with carefully planned narrative relief sculpture.

However, Sargon II met with an inglorious end. He died in battle, but this event was not perceived as a heroic act; on the contrary, the death of the king on the battlefield, which had never before occurred, was considered a sign of the wrath of the gods, whom the sovereign had evidently offended seriously. His successor Sennacherib immediately abandoned the new capital and dedicated himself wholly to the reconstruction of Nineveh, which once again became the splendid capital of the empire, partly thanks to the artistic program of the new king, who wanted to elevate the city to a status of eternal glory and make it so magnificent it would be unrivalled. Perhaps because of these prospects Sennacherib also tainted himself with terrible acts against the gods. He was very careful not to take part in the many battles he waged, which often aimed at maintaining the most important borders of the empire. Under the successor of Sargon II the territory of Assyria diminished slightly, partly because the main commitment of the king from a strategic standpoint was against Babylon. In order to end the continuous strife between rulers imposed by the Assyrians, the Chaldaean sheiks in the south and local dynasts backed by the clergy and the Elamites, Sennacherib decided to intervene in a more decisive manner. After the Elamites and Chaldaeans had kidnapped and caused the death of the crown prince Ashur-nadin-shumi, the king's decision became definitive. He decreed the total destruction of Babylon, had the great monuments demolished and flooded the city. Sennacherib also destroyed the great ziggurat, which may be identifiable as the mythical tower of Babel.

The great Assyrian king had married an Aramaean princess named Naqi'a and in Babylonian was called Zakutu, which means "pure, transparent." The new queen was quite influential in court life.

152 - A STATUE FROM NINEVEH OF A STANDING FIGURE WITH A TYPICAL HAIRDO AND BEARD WHO IS HOLDING A SPEAR (BRITISH MUSEUM, LONDON).

153 - A RELIEF SCULPTURE PORTRAIT (H. 10.9 FT/330 CM) OF KING SARGON II OF ASSYRIA FROM THE CAPITAL CITY THAT HE HAD BUILT AND THAT WAS NAMED AFTER HIM, DUR SHARRUKIN (MUSÉE DU LOUVRE, PARIS).

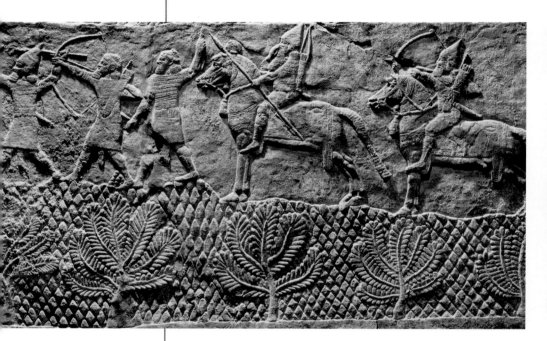

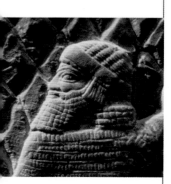

154 TOP - THE LOWER
REGISTER (H. 4.3 FT/129 CM)
OF A FRAGMENT OF A SLAB
FROM NINEVEH, DATING
FROM THE MID-7TH CENTURY
BC, ILLUSTRATES A BATTLE
SCENE WITH SOLDIERS
LAUNCHING AN ATTACK IN A
HILLY OR MOUNTAINOUS AREA
(MUSÉE DU LOUVRE, PARIS).

154 BOTTOM AND 154-155 -
THE MILITARY CAMPAIGNS
OF THE ASSYRIAN KINGS
WERE FORMIDABLE AND
EFFICIENT, AS CAN BE SEEN
IN THE UPPER REGISTER
(H. 5.4 FT/162 CM) OF A
FRAGMENT OF A SLAB RELIEF
FROM NINEVEH (MUSÉE DU
LOUVRE, PARIS).

156 - Most probably, the slabs with painted scenes of various subjects preceded the development of stone relief work. This wall painting from Tell Ahmar (h. 2 ft/65 cm; ca. 8th century BC) depicts two persons near the throne (Musée du Louvre, Paris).

157 - A gazelle (left) and a winged tutelary spirit (right) are depicted in these wall fragments (h. 20 inches/51 and 19 inches/49 cm) from Tell Ahmar, which bear witness to the level of refinement attained by Neo-Assyrian painting around the 8th century BC (Musée du Louvre, Paris).

158-159 - ASSURBANIPAL WAS THE LAST KING TO BRING SPLENDOR TO ASSYRIA. HE HAD HIMSELF PORTRAYED IN BANQUET SCENES SUCH AS THIS ONE (H. 22 INCHES/56 CM) TOGETHER WITH THE QUEEN, THE SERVANTS AND THE HEAD OF THE DEFEATED ELAMITE KING HANGING FROM A BRANCH (BRITISH MUSEUM, LONDON).

158 BOTTOM LEFT - A STELE (H. 15.25 INCHES/39 CM) REPRESENTING THE ASSYRIAN KING ASSURBANIPAL TRANSPORTING A BASKET OF BRICKS. THIS WAS A SYMBOLIC ACT OF VERY ANCIENT TRADITION AND WAS ALSO REFLECTED IN MESOPOTAMIAN LITERATURE AND MYTHOLOGY, SUCH AS IN THE POEM OF ATRAHASIS (BRITISH MUSEUM, LONDON).

158 BOTTOM RIGHT - THIS PRISM (H. 8.5 INCHES/21.5 CM) HAS A TEXT CONCERNING THE RECONSTRUCTION OF BABYLON ON THE PART OF ASARHADDON. THE KING IS WORSHIPPING WHILE FACING AN ALTAR. BEHIND HIM IS A BULL AND, IN THE LOWER REGISTER, A HILL, A PLOW AND A PALM TREE (BRITISH MUSEUM, LONDON).

Sennacherib also fell victim to a palace plot. One of his sons, who had been excluded from succession to the throne in favor of Esarhaddon, Queen Zakutu's son, organized the rebellion, but in the end it was Esarhaddon himself, supported by his mother, who reigned from 680 to 669 as king of Assyria and Babylon, which he had rebuilt. Sennacherib's successor resumed the empire's expansionist policy and led the Assyrian army into Egypt. He died during a campaign waged against the African kingdom. Under the guidance of Zakutu, the throne of Assyria was inherited by the most famous king of all, Assurbanipal, who ruled for almost 40 years (668–630? BC). He loved beauty and science. He commissioned the most impressive sculpture cycles in the realm and boasted he was a connoisseur of Sumerian and mathematics. He waged several military campaigns that were decisive and eliminated all Assyria's formidable enemies, at least for the time being, above all Elam, which unfailingly offered support to the Chaldaean tribes in their attempt to conquer Babylonia. Despite having attained such power, Assyria managed to collapse in only two decades. Assurbanipal presumably died in 630 BC and shortly afterward the empire underwent a breakdown: in 614 Cyaxares, the king of the Medes, captured Assur; in 612 Cyaxares and Nabopolassar, the Chaldaean king of Babylon, conquered Nineveh. There was still a little time left to install the last king on the throne — at Harran, where the court had fled, defended by the Egyptians — who ruled for only two years (611–609 BC). The second half of the millennium began with new powers vying for sovereignty, not only over Mesopotamia and the outlying countries, but most of Asia and the Mediterranean as well.

THE GREAT WORKS AND THE CULTURAL PROGRAM

One of the strong points in Assyrian military history was the proficiency achieved in the field of engineering science. The evolution in knowledge and experience in this sector allowed the kings to conduct victorious campaigns in all types of geographic configuration, including the conquest, albeit quite temporary, of such a large island as Cyprus, in the Mediterranean Sea. The Assyrian armies had to combat in mountainous areas, in wooded zones and on impervious passes. They had to deal with the marshland and swamps in the southern regions overlooking the Persian Gulf. They ventured into the Arabian deserts; they had to move rapidly in the foothills of Syria and Palestine; and they were able to reach the heart of such distant countries as Urartu, Elam and Egypt. The intelligent use of science and technology in that period was by no means limited to the construction of infrastructures for the troops or of the weapons and machines for sieges that we see represented on the reliefs kept in the British Muse-

um and the Louvre. The adoption of this science for civil works left an even greater mark, especially in the field of agriculture and the exploitation of the land, such as the creation of terraces that made it possible to cultivate land that could not be tilled before then. But the most striking aspect of the grandeur of the Assyrians was the realization of admirable building and urban projects. In the first half of the 9th century BC, when Assyria had just regained the power and territory that in the Middle Assyrian peri-

od ideology had been considered the minimum of the kingdom's territorial claims and had constituted the *msht Ashur* (the country of Assur), King Assurnasirpal II had a new capital designed and built. He then set about reviving in a radical manner the construction and town planning activities formerly undertaken by Shalmaneser I and Tukulti-Ninurta I. The latter had built, not far from Assur, a palace and a city called Kar-Tukulti-Ninurta (the "port of call" of Tukulti-Ninurta) on the Tigris River. His predecessor had concentrated on building a series of structures precisely at Kalakh, the site chosen by Assurnasirpal II for the construction of a sumptuous royal palace that has yielded some of the most impressive reliefs, now kept in the British Museum, London.

Assurnasirpal II was not the only ruler to inaugurate a new capital. As we have seen, over 50 years later another king, Sargon II, founded a new capital and called it Dur-Sharrukin, thus naming it after himself. His son Sennacherib once again moved the capital, this time to a traditional and "holy" place, ancient Nineveh, which had remained the undisputed fulcrum of the kingdom. Sennacherib, however, arranged and realized what was perhaps the most grandiose building and town planning project in Assyrian history, which changed the face of the centuries-old city that was sacred to Ishtar. Construction and town planning had always been central to the policy and ideology of the Assyrian rulers. We have already noted that in a certain sense this was dictated by the ecological conditions of Mesopotamia. The basis of Mesopotamian wealth was always agriculture, and the construction and maintenance of the great irrigation and canalization works was one of the primary objectives of every government in the history of Assyria and Babylonia. Besides being part of an almost obligatory plan that, as was mentioned above, resulted from the geographic and climatic conditions of the country, this building activity was obviously also a part of the economic and social programs. And it is also to be considered one of the main elements of a wide-ranging cultural program that aimed at directing the entire world toward its center which, for the Assyrians, was nothing else but the country of Assur, its capital, its palace, the king himself.

160-161 - Assyrian military power was partly due to the skill of the engineers, who built efficient war machines for sieges and attacks, as can be seen in this slab of Assurnasirpal II from Nimrud (British Museum, London).

161 - The great access gate of Nineveh during the reign of Sennacherib, which was reconstructed in modern times.

THE NEO-ASSYRIAN CAPITALS

In order to illustrate briefly the great works of the Assyrians we must return to the figure of Assurnasirpal II. At Kalakh/Nimrud, Assurnasirpal II ordered the construction of the so-called Juniper Palace, which is today known as the Northwest Palace. For the first time, at least according to the archaeological evidence at hand, we find that the palace contains decorative cycles whose purpose was to celebrate the feats of the king.

Assurnasirpal II initiated Neo-Assyrian narrative art on alabaster slabs that were to be the models for all the typical motifs of later relief work. In fact, there are three main themes in these sculptures: the exaltation of the king's might, the narration of his military exploits, and the illustration of the religious and symbolic system that revolves around the figure of the sovereign. Thus we have an area reserved for the celebration of the monarch while he is receiving the ambassadors and homage from the tributary nations, works that were carved on the slabs situated outside the great throne room, producing a striking theatrical impact. Anyone approaching the entrance of the reception area of the palace could not help being impressed, filled with pride if Assyrian, humiliated if a foreigner. The epic-narrative theme of war and hunting is mainly to be found in the reception halls, therefore inside the throne room as well. The huge hall where the king received the ambassadors and his subjects was decorated on all sides. Accompanying the heroic feats is a long cuneiform inscription that divides the scenes into two registers and describes the grand banquet that the king organized for the inauguration of the palace. Lastly, the symbolic and cult motif is to be found in different halls and in the representation of the king in the throne hall, depicted while carrying out purification rituals to the "sacred tree."

162-163 - A RELIEF (H. 34.5 INCHES/88 CM) IN THE THRONE ROOM OF ASSURNASIRPAL II SHOWING THE ASSYRIAN ARMY FORCING THE FLEEING KING OF SUHI TO SWIM TO SAFETY (BRITISH MUSEUM, LONDON).

162 BOTTOM - IN THIS RELIEF THE KING IS DEPICTED ON HIS WAR CHARIOT, WHICH IS BEING TRANSPORTED ON A BOAT (BRITISH MUSEUM, LONDON).

163 - THIS SLAB (H. 7 FT/220 CM) ILLUSTRATES THE PREPARATIONS FOR FEEDING THE SOLDIERS IN A BATTLE CAMP (BRITISH MUSEUM, LONDON).

164 AND 165 – DETAILS OF
AN ALABASTER SLAB FROM
THE RELIEFS IN THE THRONE
ROOM OF ASSURNASIRPAL II
DEPICTING AN AGITATED
BATTLE SCENE WITH VARIOUS
TYPES OF WAR MACHINES
FOR SIEGES. WAR AND
MILITARY CAMPAIGNS WERE
NOT THE ONLY SUBJECT IN
THE RELIEFS OF
ASSURNASIRPAL II, BUT THEY
PLAYED AN IMPORTANT ROLE,
ESPECIALLY IN THE
RECEPTION AND THRONE
ROOMS, WHERE THEY COULD
BE SHOWN TO THE KING'S
SUBJECTS, HIS ALLIES, AND
ALSO HIS ENEMIES (BRITISH
MUSEUM, LONDON).

166-167 - A SPLENDID REPRESENTATION
OF A ROYAL HUNT (H. 86 CM) FROM THE
THRONE ROOM OF ASSURNASIRPAL II.
THE DOMINATING CENTRAL POSITION
AND STATELINESS OF THE LION ENHANCE
THE GLORY OF THE KING (BRITISH
MUSEUM, LONDON).

168 - A WINGED SPIRIT
IS HOLDING A RECEPTACLE
FOR SPRINKLING LIQUID
AS A BENEDICTORY OR
PURIFICATORY GESTURE.
SYMBOLIC SCENES SUCH
AS THIS (H. 7.5 FT/228 CM)
WERE FREQUENTLY USED
BY ASSURNASIRPAL II
(BRITISH MUSEUM,
LONDON).

169 - A RELIEF FROM
NIMRUD (H. 5.5 INCHES/
14 CM) IN WHICH A DEMON
WITH A BIRD'S HEAD IS
PERFORMING AN ACT
OF BENEDICTION OR
PURIFICATION TOWARD THE
SACRED TREE, A HIGHLY
SYMBOLIC ELEMENT IN
NEO-ASSYRIAN CULTURE
(MUSÉE DU LOUVRE, PARIS).

170

PALACE OF SARGON II

After a period that yielded few archaeological finds, the celebrative program is documented better with Tiglath-pileser III, whose palace at Nimrud is identified with the remains of the southwest palace. But it was with Sargon II that Assyrian art reached the "classic" level. This great king, the conqueror of vast territories well beyond the typical confines of the great Mesopotamian kingdoms that had preceded him, founded a new city and made it his new capital. Horsabad (this is its modern name) is an enormous site that was called the "fortress of Sargon," *Dur Sharrukin* (*Sharru-kin*, "true king," like the mythical Sargon of Akkad), and was supposed to express the sovereign's desire for order and centralization. Officially, the city plan was presented as a work involving the construction of the temples of the Assyrian gods, but it also included the royal palace, with marvelous cycles sculpted in relief that are now in the Louvre, Paris. The town plan reveals the regularity of the edifices and infrastructures, which are mostly orthogonal. The city as a whole is an almost equilateral rectangle whose diagonals lie on North-South and East-West axes. On the side delimited by the north and east corner is the citadel, which is striking not only for its purely aesthetic value, but also for the architectural concept that lies behind it and its visual impact, which must have been awe-inspiring because of the views it afforded of the temples, the palace, the grandiose ziggurat and the network of ramps and bridges that linked the various sections.

170 LEFT - A TUTELARY SPIRIT IS DEPICTED IN THIS RELIEF (H. 7.4 FT/224 CM) PLACED ON EITHER SIDE OF THE DOORS OF THE PALACE OF ASSURNASIRPAL II AT NIMRUD. THE FIGURE WAS EXECUTED WITH A VERY THICK OUTLINE THAT HIGHLIGHTS THE POWERFUL MUSCLES (BRITISH MUSEUM, LONDON).

170 RIGHT - THIS DETAIL OF AN ALABASTER-LIMESTONE SLAB WITH A CARVED RELIEF FROM THE ROYAL PALACE OF KHORSABAD (H. 11 FT/330 CM) REPRESENTS KING SARGON II WEARING A TIARA, AND THE CROWN PRINCE (MUSÉE DU LOUVRE, PARIS).

171 - A HUMAN-HEADED BULL CARVED IN STONE (H. 13.9 FT/420 CM) FROM THE ROYAL PALACE OF KHORSABAD, ANCIENT DUR-SHARRUKIN. THE STATUE WAS MEANT TO BE VIEWED BOTH FRONTALLY AND IN PROFILE (MUSÉE DU LOUVRE, PARIS).

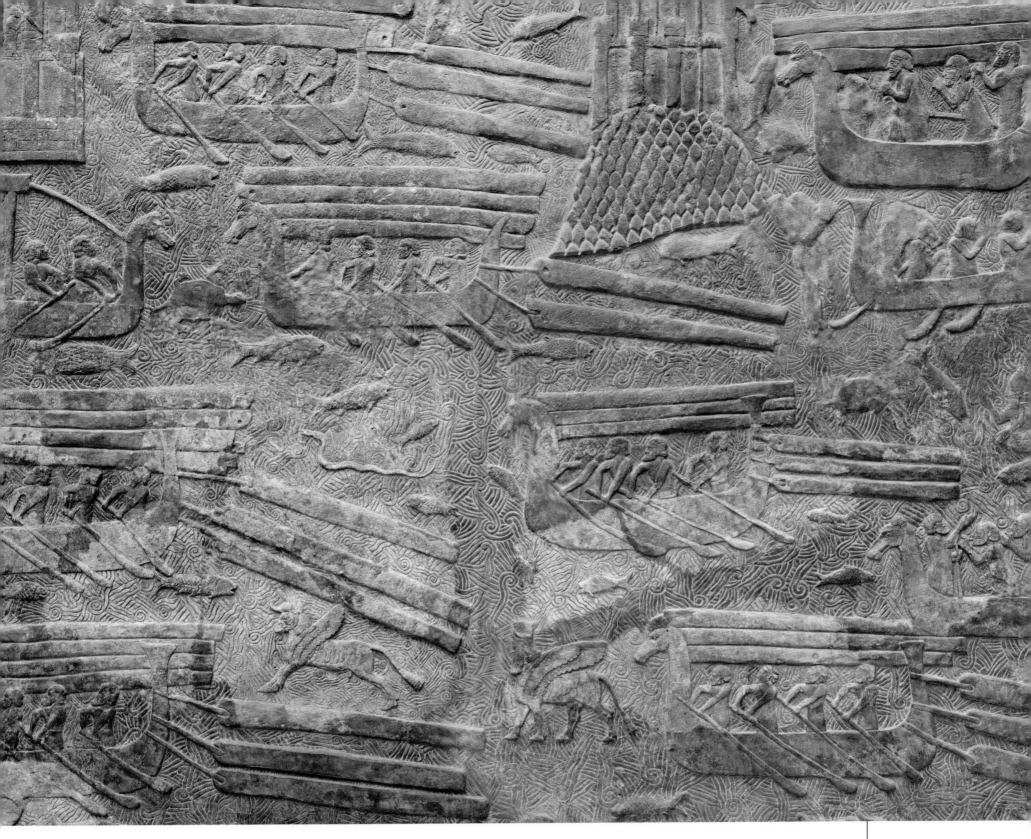

172-173 - THIS ALABASTER SLAB
(H. 15 INCHES/38 CM) FROM THE
PALACE OF KHORSABAD ILLUSTRATES
THE TRANSPORTATION OF TIMBER VIA
A WATERWAY. IN ORDER TO CONSTRUCT
THEIR PALACES, THE ASSYRIAN KINGS
GATHERED BUILDING MATERIAL FROM
ALL OVER THE NEAR EAST (MUSÉE
DU LOUVRE, PARIS).

172 BOTTOM - A DETAIL OF A RELIEF FROM
THE PALACE OF SARGON II DEPICTS A
TRIBUTARY HOLDING A MODEL OF A CITY
(MUSÉE DU LOUVRE, PARIS).

173 BOTTOM - A RELIEF (H. 6.5 FT/197 CM)
SHOWING MEN TRANSPORTING CEDAR WOOD
FOR THE CONSTRUCTION OF THE PALACE OF
SARGON II (MUSÉE DU LOUVRE, PARIS).

174 top - Detail of a relief
(h. 11.5 ft/352 cm) from
the palace of Sargon II at
Khorsabad with a scene
in which servants are
transporting gear and
supplies for the royal hunt
(Musée du Louvre, Paris).

174-175 bottom - These
details from the same relief

(h. 11.5 ft/352 cm) show
servants carrying plates
for the royal banquet and
equipment for the royal hunt
(Musée du Louvre, Paris).

175 top - Another relief (h.
11.5 ft/352 cm) with a scene
of court life: a servant
leading the royal horses
(Musée du Louvre, Paris).

PALACE OF SENNACHERIB

Sargon II initiated an imposing town planning and artistic program that his son Sennacherib set out to make his main objective, despite the fact that there had been a slackening of control in the territories his father had recently conquered. Sennacherib presented himself as the one who again founded the very ancient city of Nineveh, whose immense construction and hydraulic engineering works would establish him as the dominator of nature as well as of peoples. Now, with its new abundant supply of water Nineveh was able to host animal reserves and parks with exotic plants, which

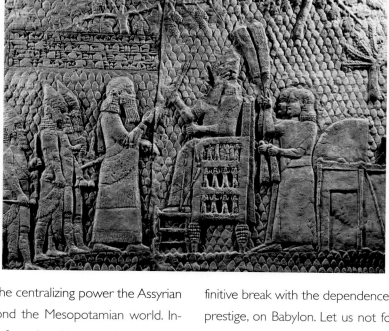

again served to underscore the centralizing power the Assyrian monarch wielded even beyond the Mesopotamian world. Indeed, according to a recently formulated hypothesis, it is possible that the famous hanging gardens of Babylon were tradition-

ally attributed to the southern capital by mistake, because of the confusion between Nineveh and Babylon that is evinced in biblical texts as well, and that they were really located in the Assyrian capital. Herodotus' eloquent silence regarding the hanging gardens after his visit to Babylon certainly makes a strong case in favor of this hypothesis. The palace that Sennacherib had built and adorned with great relief cycles that are now in the British Museum was called the "incomparable palace." Certainly the king, by founding Nineveh again on such a monumental and "incomparable" scale, pursued a policy of a definitive break with the dependence, both in terms of culture and prestige, on Babylon. Let us not forget that the counterpart of the grandiose works at Nineveh was the destruction of the Babylonian capital.

176 - THIS RELIEF (H. 6 FT/182 CM) IS PART OF A DECORATIVE CYCLE IN THE PALACE OF SENNACHERIB AT NINEVEH. THE DETAIL SHOWS ONE OF THE MOMENTS IN THE BATTLE OF LACHISH IN PALESTINE. THIS EPISODE WAS CELEBRATED TO QUITE A DEGREE BY SENNACHERIB, WHO WAS GENERALLY NOT CONSIDERED A MILITARY LEADER (BRITISH MUSEUM, LONDON).

177 TOP - A RELIEF IN WHICH KING SENNACHERIB IS RECEIVING THE HOMAGE OF THE ENEMY KING AFTER THE BATTLE OF LACHISH (BRITISH MUSEUM, LONDON).

177 BOTTOM - THIS DETAIL SHOWS ASSYRIAN SOLDIERS ATTACKING THE CITY OF LACHISH (BRITISH MUSEUM, LONDON).

HISTORY AND TREASURES OF AN ANCIENT CIVILIZATION

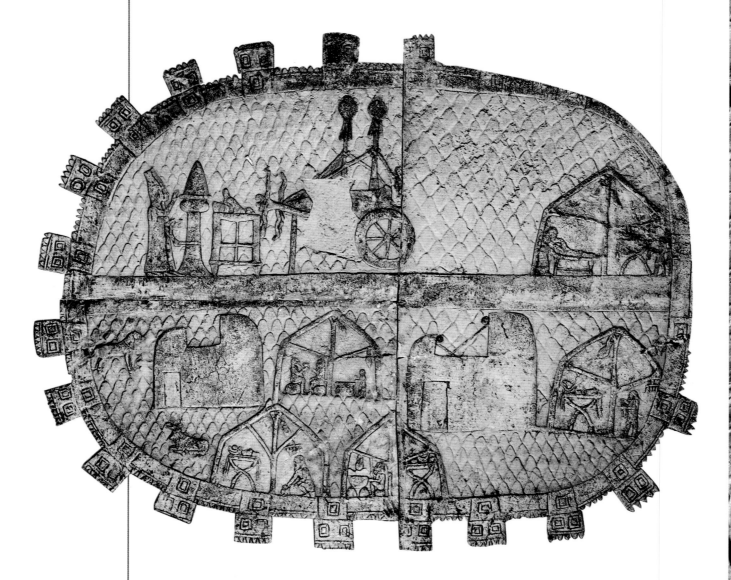

178 AND 179 - DETAILS FROM THE CYCLE OF SCULPTURE RELIEFS DEDICATED TO THE LACHISH CAMPAIGN: AN ASSYRIAN SOLDIER LEADING PRISONERS (P. 178 ABOVE), THE ASSYRIAN CAMP FORTIFIED DURING THE SIEGE OF THE CITY (P. 178 BELOW), AND A SCENE OF EXILES BEING DEPORTED (PP. 178-179). DEPORTATION WAS A METHOD ADOPTED BY THE ASSYRIAN KINGS IN AN ATTEMPT TO SUBJUGATE THE COUNTRIES THEY HAD CONQUERED (BRITISH MUSEUM, LONDON).

180-181 - A detail of the reliefs illustrating the Battle of Lachish that shows exiles being deported (at left) while some Assyrian soldiers are torturing and probably killing some of the defeated enemies, perhaps Nubians (British Museum. London).

181 - Another detail showing the victorious Assyrian soldiers impaling their enemies under the walls of Lachish (British Museum, London).

PALACE OF ASSURBANIPAL

Esarhaddon resumed Assyrian expansionism, while as to construction works, he concentrated on rebuilding Babylon. The last great Assyrian king, Assurbanipal, effected an anti-Babylonian policy that aimed mainly at increasing the cultural influence of Nineveh. The new king was fond of boasting about his high level of culture and, besides having a new palace (the North Palace) built and decorated, he accumulated the largest collection of pre-classical antiquity in a library that was also used as a study center. This institution has yielded many of the documents that have provided information regarding the ancient Assyrian, Babylonian and Sumerian civilizations, because Assurbanipal wanted to collect documents concerning all Mesopotamian culture from its origin and in all its various manifestations: encyclopedias, poems, rituals, treatises and so forth. The great narrative cycles sculpted in relief that Assurbanipal commissioned reveal the personality of this king, portraying him in scenes of court life and moments of leisure, engaged in battles and while hunting wild animals. From the reign of Tiglathpileser III on, the subjects of these sculpture cycles concentrated on epic-narrative themes, to the detriment mostly of symbolic and cult representations. The war and hunting motifs also offered the artists the possibility of creating a unified development by means of long and coherent cycles. These works provide us with a great deal of information and documentation of the world at that time. There are the tools and objects used for various tasks, as well as the clothes people wore then. We see how the Assyrians waged war, how they performed their rituals, and how they punished their defeated enemies. The reliefs also show the technique adopted by the Assyrians to transport the colossal bulls that flanked the city gates and palace entrances. Naturally, there are not only the Assyrians, but the other populations of the time as well. These include Phoenicians drowning in the sea; Elamite soldiers trying to save their wounded companions, or others asking the Assyrians who have defeated them to be merciful and slay them.

182 - A MID-7TH CENTURY BC RELIEF (H. 3.9 FT/114 CM) FROM NINEVEH IN WHICH THE CROWN PRINCE OF ASSURBANIPAL IS KILLING A LION (BRITISH MUSEUM, LONDON).

183 AND 184-185 - ASSURBANIPAL COMMISSIONED HIGHLY ELEGANT RELIEFS WITH BATTLE AND HUNTING SCENES (MAX. H. 5 FT/152 CM; BRITISH MUSEUM. LONDON).

186 - The being with a body that is half-human and half-lion in this relief is one of the many demons and protective spirits that decorated the palaces of the Assyrian kings (British Museum, London).

186-187 - This splendid detail (h. 5 ft/157 cm) depicts a protective demon that represents the symbolic-religious tradition in Assyrian relief art (British Museum, London).

HISTORY AND TREASURES OF AN ANCIENT CIVILIZATION

188-189 - AMONG THE FINE RELIEFS IN
THE NORTH PALACE OF NINEVEH, THE
PALACE OF ASSURBANIPAL, THERE ARE
EXCITING REPRESENTATIONS OF BATTLE
SCENES, SUCH AS THE ONE OF A WAR
CHARIOT WITH A PAIR OF HORSES,
A CHARIOTEER AND ARCHERS (H. 3.5
FT/110 CM; MUSÉE DU LOUVRE, PARIS).

190 - AMONG THE VICTORIOUS WARS THAT ASSURBANIPAL CELEBRATED IN THE SCULPTURE CYCLES IS THE ONE AGAINST ELAM. THIS RELIEF ILLUSTRATES THE CAPTURE OF HADAMU, WITH THE ASSYRIAN SOLDIERS DESTROYING THE WALLS OF THE CITY (BRITISH MUSEUM, LONDON).

191 - ASSURBANIPAL ALSO WAGED WAR AGAINST THE ARABS. IN THIS FRAGMENT OF AN ALABASTER RELIEF (H. 4.5 FT/135 CM) ONE CAN SEE THE HEAD OF A CAMEL, AN ANIMAL USED IN THE BATTLES AGAINST THE ASSYRIANS (BRITISH MUSEUM, LONDON).

192-193 - THE SIEGE OF AN EGYPTIAN CITY IS ILLUSTRATED IN THIS RELIEF SCULPTURE (H. 3.9 FT/114 CM) FROM NINEVEH (BRITISH MUSEUM, LONDON).

194-195 - A RELIEF SHOWING THE ELAMITES SURRENDERING TO THE ASSYRIANS (BRITISH MUSEUM, LONDON).

196-197 - An tumultuous scene of Elamite soldiers fleeing after an attack by Assurbanipal's army is the subject of this relief from the palace of Nineveh (British Museum, London).

197 - In this relief the marching Assyrian army is dragging the Elamite king, who was taken prisoner at the end of the battle. With the conquest of Elam and Egypt, Assyria became the master of the entire Near East (British Museum, London).

THE "STATE ARCHIVES"

The Assyrian monarchs have told the story of their adventure not only through art, but have also left the "state archives," which provide us with detailed descriptions of the society and history of the time. The types of texts kept in the archives include letters, bookkeeping registers, legal texts, treatises, written agreements and divinatory texts. The last-mentioned documents are important because the Assyrian kings, especially the last ones, were interested in understanding the signs the gods had left in various natural phenomena. The art of divination had played a fundamental role in Mesopotamian society already in the III Millennium BC, so that this was by no means an original development. Yet the cultural spirit of the Assyrian monarchs was distinguished by the obsessive attention they paid to the possession, care and use of documents regarding divination. In this context, the main field was astrology; this was the art the monarchs turned to the most, also favoring it over the others as far as study and preservation were concerned. At the time astrology was more a science than a mere collection of opinions expressed by charlatans. Before the Neo-Assyrian period, a great deal of effort had been made to establish a categorical order for the diverse observations of phenomena made in different epochs and places. The result of this labor was a series of long, well-ordered lists of phenomena with the respective oracular responses that had been perpetuated by tradition. Since these responses referred to events and realities that no longer existed, in order to make use of the presages it was necessary to consult experts who were able to interpret the old response in the light of the new situation. For example, these experts had to know how to find a contemporary king, country or other reality that would correspond to the "country of Amurru," which no longer existed. Leaving aside the purely magical aspect, the study of astrological texts and of divination produced philological activity bent on verifying the state of preservation of the tablets and the quality of the text written on them. The Assyrian kings had at their disposal a vast network to compile texts and gradually group them in their libraries, thus forming impressive collections. Within the context of this program the foundations were being laid for the study of celestial phenomena based on calculation that in the following centuries would become typical and would contribute to the establishment of the description of the cosmos according to rational Greek geometry.

198 - THIS TABLET (H. 7 INCHES/17.15 CM) IS A COPY MADE FOR THE LIBRARY OF ASSURBANIPAL AT NINEVEH. IT CONTAINS ASTRONOMIC OBSERVATIONS OF THE PLANET VENUS, ON THE BASIS OF WHICH SCHOLARS ARE NOW ATTEMPTING TO RECONSTRUCT AN ABSOLUTE CHRONOLOGY OF MESOPOTAMIAN HISTORY (BRITISH MUSEUM, LONDON).

To conclude this section given over to the cultural programs of the Assyrians, mention should be made of the role played by the god Assur and his "governor" and high priest, the king. Already in the Middle Assyrian period the god of the city of Assur was gradually associated with Enlil first, and then An and Anshar, ancestors of Enlil and Marduk (let us not forget that Marduk, in Babylonian tradition, had replaced Enlil as the king of the gods). Assur was not only the tutelary god of the city because of the particular historic-social tradition of Assyria as we know it from the ancient period on. He was also the symbol of Assyrian unity and the Assyrian community, and represented the deepest root of the large-scale imperial expansion of this people. With time, the sense of unity among the god, the city, the community that lived in it and the king was transformed into a symbol of totality, the totalizing spirit that pursued the unification of Mesopotamia and then of the entire civilized world. Assur gradually became a god with "exclusive" features: he was venerated only in the holy city that bore his name and which he ruled as king. The Assyrian monarchs would always be the kings *of the land* of Assur, never kings of the *city* of Assur. It was as if, once having taken on the role of administrator on behalf of the god, the king could count on divine investiture to conquer lands that, however, already belonged to Assur and the gods of Assyria. He thus became the king of a territory that was already Assur's but had to be conquered again in conformity with his will. The exclusive features of the god Assur have led scholars to think there may have been monotheistic traditions in the cultured upper classes of society. Indeed, we have much evidence that shows that the sages were divided into "circles," the most important of which was the "inner circle," made up of the leading experts in "secret knowledge," that is to say, divination and the art of writing, as well as astrology, which as we have seen had the greatest influence on the king. It may be that the figure of the king as the sole sovereign in the world was accompanied by increasingly marked symbolism of Assur as the chief divine principle, of which the other gods were nothing else but manifestations or aspects along the path toward true knowledge.

Without a doubt the Neo-Assyrian cultural program is one of the most fascinating mysteries in ancient civilization, above all because of its possible links with the esoteric wisdom of Palestine, of the Median and Persian Magi, and even of the Greek philosophers. Scholars are still struggling to comprehend and explain this mystery as best they can, for despite the possibilities provided by the rich documentation available, it is quite fragmentary and complex. In any case, what emerges quite clearly is that there are certain similarities to, and even dependence upon, the roots of Western civilization, as well as a great distance between the two cultures.

THE THEOLOGY, POLITICS AND "ESOTERICISM" OF ASSUR

199 - This tablet is an example of a literary text preserved in Nineveh. It contains part of the myth of Etana, the ancient Sumerian king who ascended to the sky on an eagle's back (British Museum, London).

THE FINAL BABYLONIAN EXPLOIT AND THE PERSIAN CONQUEST

During the rapid disintegration of the empire, the Chaldean king Nabopolassar took control of Babylon and, aided by Cyaxares, the king of the Medes, set about fighting against the empire. For Assyria this was the end, as the cities were destroyed and the population fled from the countryside. However, Babylon gained virtual dominion over all the Assyrian territory as if it were a natural succession, so much so that it was mistaken for Nineveh in the biblical texts. Nebuchadnezzar II, another dominating figure in the imagination of the Western World and in the history of Babylonia, in his 40 years of rule extended the borders to the west and south, where he came into contact with the new and developing Arab civilizations. To the north and east new dangerous powers were making their presence felt: the Medes had gained control of a vast empire between Iran and Turkey, but in a short time the Persians under Cyrus II (Cyrus the Great) became the masters of an empire of unheard-of dimensions, by annexing the vast kingdom of the Medes and by arriving at the Mediterranean via Turkey with the conquest of Lydia, ruled by Croesus. The Persians had already filled the power vacuum left by the Elamites in the southern regions. Thus, Babylon was soon completely surrounded. King Nabonedo, who succeeded Nebuchadnezzar II after a period marked by the rapid alternation of rather weak kings, seemed hardly interested in the emerging threat on the part of the Persians. Nabonedo was yet another example of an "anonymous" and "non-conformist" king. He was strenuously opposed by the priests of the god Marduk, partly because of his behavior, which was unique at the time. Indeed, Nabonedo even went so far as to reproach Marduk for having abandoned some Babylonian cities, allowing them to be destroyed by the Medes during the period of their war against Assyria. Like the other kings who opposed tradition, Nabonedo founded a new capital in an Arab zone, at Teima, and then strongly supported and amplified the cult of the astral divinities Sin, Shamash and Ishtar. The cities that housed the principal sanctuaries of these gods took on new importance: Harran, above all, the city of the sanctuary of Sin, which had been destroyed by the Medes. All this took place under the influence of the king's mother Adad-Guppi, who had been a priestess of Sin at Harran. The year 539 BC marked the end of Babylonian civilization as a politically independent entity. Cyrus the Great entered Babylon with the approval of the clergy and much to his amazement found one of the must luxurious cities in all antiquity. The feverish construction activity of Nebuchadnezzar II had made Babylon worthy of its long-standing desire to be known as the center of the world. Monuments such as the Gate of Ishtar, the so-called Tower of Babel and the Hanging Gardens left an unforgettable impression on ancient visitors, and to this day we cannot but be awestruck upon observing the reconstruction of the Gate of Ishtar or the various models of the Tower of Babel.

200 - CARVED IN THIS CLAY TABLET (H. 5 INCHES/12.2 CM) IS A MAP THAT SHOWS THE BABYLONIANS' CONCEPTION OF THE SHAPE OF THE EARTH. IN THE MIDDLE IS BABYLON, AROUND WHICH ARE THE FOREIGN COUNTRIES, THE MOUNTAINS AND THE OCEAN (BRITISH MUSEUM, LONDON).

201 - A DECORATIVE FRIEZE DATING FROM THE 7TH CENTURY BC AND MADE OF GLAZED AND ENAMELED BRICKS, FOUND IN THE THRONE ROOM OF THE SOUTH PALACE OF BABYLON (VORDERASIATISCHES MUSEUM, BERLIN).

202-203 - THIS DETAIL OF ENAMELED BRICKS (H. 41 INCHES/105 CM) FROM THE PROCESSIONAL ROAD NEAR THE GATE OF ISHTAR DEPICTS A ROARING LION (MUSÉE DU LOUVRE, PARIS).

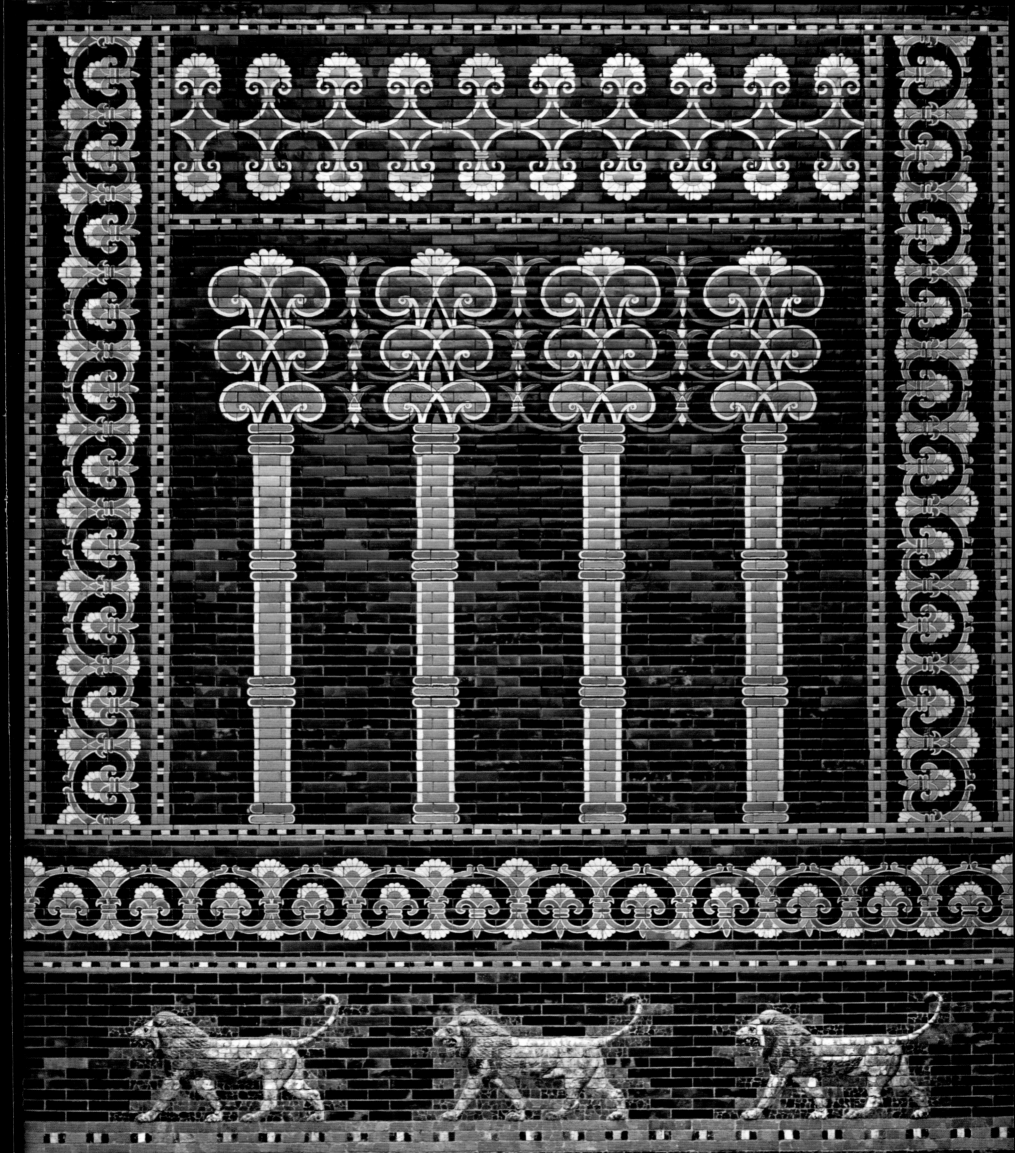

INDEX

HISTORY AND TREASURES OF AN ANCIENT CIVILIZATION

BIBLIOGRAPHY

Biga M. G., *I Babilonesi*. Carocci, Rome 2004.

Bottéro J., *Mesopotamie. L'ecriture, la raison et les dieux*. Gallimard, Paris 1987

Bottéro J., Kramer N., *Lorsque les dieux faisaient l'homme: mythologie mesopotamienne*. Gallimard, Paris 1990.

Ceram C. W., *Götter, Gräber und Gelehrte. Roman der Archäologie*. Rowohlt 1967.

Fales F. M., *L'impero assiro. Storia e amministrazione, 9.-7. secolo a. C.* Laterza, Rome-Bari 2001.

Invernizzi A., *Dal Tigri all'Eufrate*. Le Lettere, Florence 1992 (2 vols.).

Margueron J.-C., *Les Mesopotamiens*. Armand Colin,Paris 1991.

Klengel H., *Konig Hammurapi und der Alltag Babylons*. Artemis, Zurich 1991.

Liverani M., *Antico Oriente. Storia, società, economia*. Laterza, Bari 1988.

Matthiae P., *La storia dell'arte dell'Oriente Antico. Gli stati territoriali 2100-1600*. Electa, Milan 2000.

Matthiae P., *La storia dell'arte dell'Oriente Antico. I primi imperi e i principati del Ferro 1600-700*. Electa, Milan 1997.

Matthiae P., *La storia dell'arte dell'Oriente Antico. I grandi imperi 1000-330*. Electa, Milan 1996.

Matthiae P., *Il sovrano e l'opera*. Laterza, Bari 1994.

Matthiae P., *L'arte degli Assiri*. Laterza, Rome-Bari 1996.

Matthiae P., *Ninive*. Electa, Milan 1998.

McAdams R., *The Evolution of Urban Society*, Chicago 1966

Nissen H. J., *Gurndzüge einer Geschichte der Frühzeit des Vorderen Orients*, Darmstadt 1983.

Oppenheim A. L., *Ancient Mesopotamia*, Chicago 1977.

von Soden W., *Einfuhurung in die Altorientalistik*. Wissenschaftliche Buchges, Darmstadt 1985.

Pettinato G., *Babilonia. Centro dell'universo*. Rusconi, Milan 1994.

Pettinato G., *Mitologia sumerica*. UTET, Turin 2001.

Pettinato G., *La saga di Gilgamesh*. Mondadori, Milan 2004.

Pettinato G., *Mitologia assiro-babilonese*. UTET, Turin 2005.

Pettinato G., *Angeli e demoni a Babilonia. Magia e mito nelle antiche civiltà mesopotamiche*. Mondadori, Milan 2001.

Pettinato G., *La scrittura celeste. La nascita dell'astrologia in Mesopotamia*. Mondadori, Milan 1999.

Saporetti C., *Antiche leggi. I «Codici» del Vicino Oriente antico*. Rusconi, Milan 1998.

Saporetti C., *Come sognavano gli antichi*. Rusconi, Milan 1999.

PHOTO CREDITS

208 - A RELIEF (H. 224 CM) FROM THE PALACE OF ASSURNASIRPAL II AT NIMRUD ILLUSTRATING A WINGED SPIRIT HOLDING A GOAT AND AN EAR OF WHEAT (BRITISH MUSEUM, LONDON).